Major Religions of the World

MAJOR RELIGIONS OF THE WORLD

by
MAX STILSON

ZONDERVAN PUBLISHING HOUSE
GRAND RAPIDS, MICHIGAN

Library of Congress Catalog Card No. 64-11951

Printed in the United States of America

INTRODUCTION

My interest in the religions of the world began during World War II when I was stationed with the 18th Field Hospital in Iran (Persia) and India, the birthplaces of many of the world's religions.

The customs, doctrines and practices of these religions were strange to one who had been born and reared in America.

Since the end of World War II, the religions of the world have become no longer foreign to the Americans. The rapid means of communication have brought these religions much nearer to America. Many of these religions have become newsworthy as the beliefs and practices of certain sects have largely determined national policy in some countries.

The rapid means of transportation have brought many Americans into contact with the religions of the East. Many Americans now spend their vacations on foreign soil. This was possible only for the wealthy a few years ago.

There has been an increase in the number of foreign students who have come to America for education. About 100,000 foreign students are now studying in our universities to return to their homelands as engineers, doctors, scientists, teachers, etc. They are ardent missionaries of their faith. Many of them for the first time are able to observe Christianity at work. And many Christian students have their first contact with those of the Eastern faiths.

The International Students, Inc., 2627 Connecticut Avenue, Washington 8, D.C. is a non-profit Christian organization which is dedicated to reaching these foreign students with the Gospel of Christ. Many have been won to Christ and have returned to their homelands as faithful witnesses of the power of Christ in the individual life.

Many of the Eastern religions have looked to America as a ripe mission field. They have seen the indifference of many Christians and have moved into America and are gaining many converts and building their temples and mosques throughout America.

Many Americans do not understand the beliefs or strange practices of the religions of the world. This book is not intended to be a detailed guide to the religions but is intended to be an elementary study which will give the basic history and beliefs of these religions. The student will then be able to advance to a more detailed study of each religion by using the books listed for further study.

The missionary programs of our churches have been left largely in the hands of the women of the church. The men who are the leaders of our churches should be familiar with the religions of the world so that they may be able to teach others also.

Study that you might be a better workman who need not to be ashamed due to lack of knowledge. Knowledge is power and the Christian should be fully informed concerning these religions and their work.

The study of religions is interesting and will readily prove the superiority of Christianity over the other religions of the world.

MAX STILSON

Phoenix, Arizona

CONTENTS

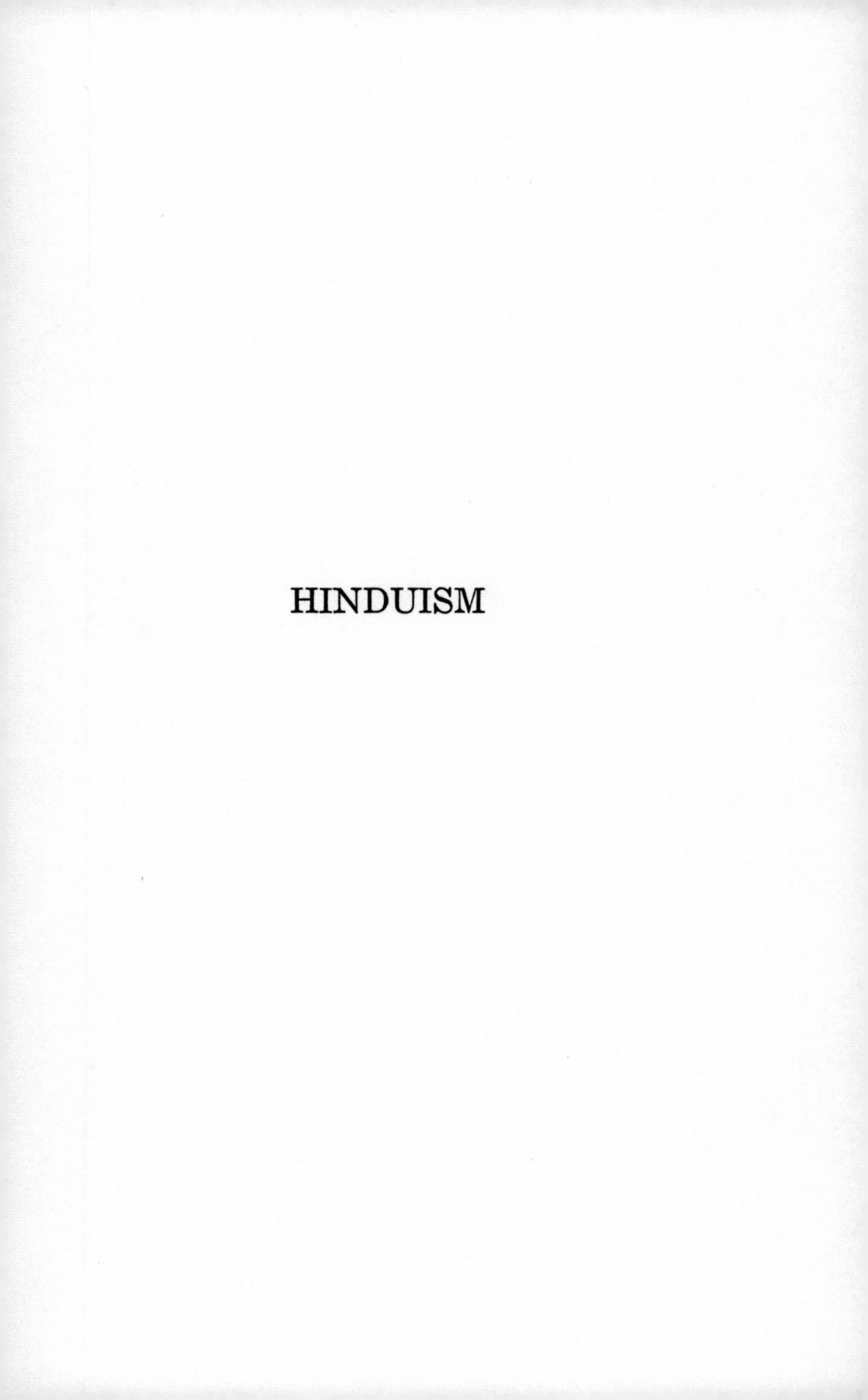

HINDUISM

Chapter 1

HINDUISM

Hinduism is believed to be the oldest of the existing religions. It is many thousands of years old. The founding of Hinduism has been traced to India but no individual founder has been found.

The Hindus use many sacred books but the best known are: The Vedas, The Brahmanas, and The Upanishads.

There are many sects of Hinduism which vary in doctrine and ritual and no study will exhaust all the sects which have their own temples, dress differently and observe different religious holydays. All the sects, however, accept the doctrines of reincarnation and Nirvana.

Gorinda Dar, a Hindu writer, has defined Hinduism: "No definition is possible, for the very good reason that Hinduism is absolutely indefinite. It is really an anthopological process to which, by a strange irony of fate, the name of 'religion' has been given. Starting from the Vedas, embodying the customs and ideas of one or a few tribes, it has like a snowball gone on ever getting bigger and bigger in the course of ages, as it has steadily gone on absorbing from the customs and ideas of all people with whom it has come into contact, down to the present day. It rejects nothing. It is all-comprehensive, all-absorbing, all-tolerant, all-complacent, all-compliant. Every type of mind can derive nourishment from it. It has its spiritual and esoteric, its subjective and objective, its rational and irrational, its pure and impure aspects."

Many reformers of Hinduism have added new ideas and beliefs. Some have sought to change old beliefs while others have established new religions such as Buddha and Mahavira, which will be discussed later.

Hinduism is the only religion in the world which believes in the holiness of the castes. Originally there were only four castes: Brahmans or priests; warriors; merchants and traders; and Sudras, which includes all those who are not members of the other three castes. Members of a higher caste may not eat or drink with a member of a lower caste. They may not enter the same temple. They may not let their children play together. They may not marry outside of their caste. As recently as 1948 a bill was passed in the Indian Constituent Assembly which abolished this "untouchability" and forbade its practice.

The essentials of Hinduism can be summed up as follows:

1. Belief in the doctrine of Karma, or the law of the dead.
2. Belief in the transmigration of souls.
3. A consequent general pessimistic view of life and the desire to find release.
4. A high regard for the ascetic.
5. A dominant emphasis on the passive virtues.
6. A deep reverence for the Vedas.
7. An underlying pantheism.
8. An esteem for the practice of the Dharma, law, usage, custom.
9. Observance of the principles of caste.

Eight hundred years ago India was invaded by Mohammedanism. The Moslems came with swords instead of arguments in favor of their system. They put many Hindus, who would not accept Mohammedanism, to death. The Hindus accepted the Mohammedan's belief in one God as opposed to the many gods which they were worshiping.

Five hundred years ago a Brahmin widow in Benares had a son whom she placed in a basket afloat on a lotus pond. A Mohammedan weaver, Niau, and his wife, Nina, found the basket and brought it home. They named the boy, Kabir. He was sent to the best teachers in Benares. He liked to study. When he was sixteen years old, he had studied both Mohammedanism and Hinduism. He became acquainted with the work of the poet, Ramanand, who taught the doctrine of one God and that truth is man's greatest friend, and living the simple life is the way to Nirvana.

Kabir also became a weaver and he composed poems of what people ought to believe and do to lead a good life. He became famous as a poet although he continued to earn his living as a weaver.

He attended the purification rites of the Hindus washing their sins away in their sacred river, the Ganges. He preached the doctrine of one God to the Hindu priests. Through his poems, he gained many followers. He believed that the priests and monks ought to work to support themselves and he set the example.

His poetry warned against pride and vanity. He preached against the caste system of India and against the worship of idols.

Kabir died in Maghar and the Hindus claimed that he belonged to them while the Mohammedans made the same claim. His poetry was collected into the book *Bijak* and his followers called themselves Kabir Panthis or followers of the Kabir path. The *Bijak* became the holy scriptures of Kabir Panthis.

Guru Nanak was the son of a noble Hindu and his pious wife. He was born when the poet Kabir was thirty years old. His father was a poor man who tried to give his son a good education. Nanak began to study Persian and Arabic when he was nine years old. He became interested in religion but he disliked work of any kind.

If his parents found a wife for Nanak, he would have to earn his own living — but he refused to work. He day-dreamed about the religion of his people and read the poetry of Ramanand and Kabir. Nanak was thirty years old when he announced that he was a Guru or a teacher of a new religion. He declared that both the teachings of Mohammedanism and Hinduism were wrong. He preached one God, opposed the caste system, and preached that it was sinful to worship idols.

Kabir had taught that people ought not to eat meat. Nanak taught that people could eat meat if the animal was slain with one blow of the sword.

Nanak teamed up with a servant, Mordana, who was a beautiful singer. They attracted large crowds around the market-places.

Nanak died at the age of 70. A man named Angad became the next Guru. Other Gurus followed and the fifth Guru, Arjan, collected the sayings and sermons of Nanak, the poems of Ramanand and Kabir into a book which he called Granth Sabeb, the holy scriptures of Nanak, which religion he called Sikhism. Arjan had little success in spreading his new religion and organized an army to spread his teachings by the sword.

Guru Har succeeded Arjan and organized his followers and started a war against the Mohammedans. A hundred years later the Sikhs established an independent kingdom which today boasts of three million followers, mostly soldiers.

The five Kukkas of Sikhism are:

1. Kes — long hair
2. Kunga — wooden comb in the hair
3. Kach — white drawer worn next to the skin

4. Kara — iron bracelet
5. Khanda — short two-edged dagger which is always worn in the streets.

Sikhism required its followers to comb their hair at least twice a day, bathe often and read their holy scriptures daily. The Holy City of Sikhism is Amritsar. Its temple is called the Golden Temple in the Pool of Immortality. Its holy scriptures are placed on the altar and worshiped.

Dayananda was the son of a high caste Hindu. He received the sacred thread and was sent to the best teachers in the land, with whom he studied languages and religion for six years.

Dayananda's father wanted him to keep the Fast of Shivarati which is kept by all Hindus who worship the god Shiva. All Hindus worship the three-in-one God but they also worship each one of the three separately. Some worship one of the three more than the others, and it seems that Shiva has the greatest number of followers. His followers have many holydays and fasts. During the Fast of Shivarati, the people fasted a night, a day and another night. The first night the people sat up all night in the Temple of Shiva singing hymns. The worshipers fell asleep and Dayananda noticed a mouse which was drinking the wine which was offered to Shiva. This shook his faith in the idol.

To attempt to stop his study of religion, his parents arranged a wedding for Dayananda. He delayed but his father finally forced him to set a day. A few days before the wedding, Dayananda disappeared. He changed his name and put on the clothes of a beggar. He sought a teacher who could teach him the truth about religion. He wandered through India, studying under many learned men, but none satisfied him.

Dayananda went to the Hindu sacred river, Ganges, to study under the holy men there. He found a teacher who hated idols and taught Dayananda about the teachings of Rajah Rammohan Roy and the assembly of God. Rammohan Roy had not been satisfied with the teachings of the Hindus. He was a great scholar and had studied Arabic, Persian, Sanskrit and Hebrew, even making a careful study of the Bible under Christian missionaries. He found some teachings of the Bible which he liked very much. These he combined with the teachings of other religions.

Dayananda studied the Bible and the writings of Rajah Rammohan Roy for two years. He became convinced that one ought to worship one God instead of the many gods of the Hindus. He was also convinced that there are no castes by birth as some people are born more intelligent than others. He believed in repentance for the forgiveness of sins by God. But he still believed in Reincarnation and Nirvana as taught by the Hindus. He organized his followers into a sect called Arja Samaj (the assembly of the Noble) in 1875 when he was 51 years old. Eight years later he died and today his sect has millions of followers.

There are several teachings which are common to nearly all Hindus:

The cow is regarded as sacred by the Hindus.

Mahatma Gandhi said, "Cow-protection is to me one of the most wonderful phenomena in human evolution. It takes the human being beyond his species. The cow to me means the entire sub-human world. Man through the cow is enjoined to realize his identity with all that lives. She is the mother to millions of Indian mankind. The cow is a poem of pity. Protection of the cow means protection of the whole dumb creation of God."

Monier-Williams wrote, "The cow is of all animals the most sacred. Every part of its body is inhabited by some deity or other. Every hair on its body is inviolable, all its excreta are hallowed. Not a particle ought to be thrown away as impure. On the contrary, the water it ejects ought to be preserved as the best of all holy waters — a sin-destroying liquid which sanctifies everything it touches, while nothing purifies like cow-dung. Any spot which a cow has condescended to honor with the sacred deposit of her excrement is forever afterwards consecrated ground, and the filthiest place plastered with it is at once cleansed and freed from pollution, while the ashes produced by burning this hallowed substance are of such a holy nature, that they not only make clean all material things, however previously unclean, but have only to be sprinkled over a sinner to convert him into a saint."

The killing of cows in times past merited capital punishment. Men are still outcast for it. This is the major source of conflict between the Moslems and the Hindus. Cows receive the honor that should be given to deities. Garlands are placed around their necks, oil is poured on their foreheads and water on their feet. Cow-dung is used as a fuel and as a disinfectant element dissolved in water used to wash the floors, thresholds and walls. It is used as an ingredient in clay-mortar, mud plaster and as a medicine.

The Hindu woman has never been accepted as an equal by the man, although reforms in recent years have elevated the status of the Hindu woman.

Padmapurana, a Hindu writer, wrote, "There is no other god on earth for a woman than her husband. The most excellent of all good works that she can do is to seek to please him by manifesting perfect obedience to him. Therein should be her sole rule of life.

"Be her husband deformed, aged, infirm, offensive in his manner; let him be choleric, debauched, immoral, a drunkard, a gambler, let him frequent places of ill-repute, live in open sin with other women, have no affection for his home, let him rave like a lunatic, let him live without home; let him be blind, deaf, dumb, or crippled; in a word, let his defects be what they may, a wife must always look upon him as her god, should lavish him with all her affection and care, paying no heed whatsoever to his character and giving him no cause whatsoever for disapproval.

"A wife must eat only after her husband has had his fill. If the latter fasts, she shall fast, too; if he touch not food, she also shall not touch it; if he be in affliction, she shall be so, too; if he be cheerful, she shall share his joy. She must be on the death of her husband willing to allow herself to be burnt alive on the same funeral pyre; then everybody will praise her virtue." The last quotation which is known as Sutter, is now outlawed but is often practiced in isolated villages in spite of every precaution of the police.

Child marriages were practiced by the Hindus for centuries. This practice was traced to a family law of the fifth century B.C. which required the marriage of all girls before puberty. Many widows through the Code of Manu were never allowed to remarry. They were forced to spend long years of widowhood which was a burden on the family. Widowers were allowed to remarry and this led to unequal marriages between middle-aged men and child wives. A child marriage Restraint Bill was passed in 1930 which prohibited marriages of girls under 14 and boys under 18, but this was confined to British India.

The Code of Manu was a collection of rules of life which was passed in 200 B.C. and observed by many Hindus. It laid great stress on the ceremonies which should surround the life of each individual and accompany him from birth to death and beyond. The Hindu must observe all rules of his caste. He was never allowed to marry outside of it. He must never break any of the strict dietary laws and social regulations laid down for it. He must be faithful in performing for himself and others many religious rites and ceremonies. The Code of Manu prescribes for each individual a long list of sacramental rites for each significant episode of life — at birth, at name-giving, at first taking out to see the sun, at first feeding with boiled rice, at first hair cutting, at initiation into manhood, at marriage, etc.

There are several systems of Orthodox Hindu philosophy which were developed between 500 B.C. and A.D. 500.

1. *Sankhya System*

This system was founded by Kapile about a century before Buddha and profoundly influenced both Jainism and Buddhism. It is staunchly dualistic and theistic. It teaches that there are two categories of beings: (1) matter or the phenomenal world, (2) soul – an infinite number of individual souls which are each independent and eternal. Souls entangled in nature have fallen into misery and suffering through ignorance of the distinction between soul and matter which have led directly to the fettering of the soul to bodily processes and to nature which causes the soul to be reborn again and again.

2. *The Yoga System*

This is a system of mental discipline. It has become highly developed since its introduction in the Upanishads. Patanjah in the second century A.D. highly refined the techniques of Yoga. He derived most of his ideas from the Sankhya system but accepted theism as part of his world view.

There are eight steps in the Yoga system:

1. Performing the five desires – killing vows or Yama; a step by which the Yoga aspirant abstains from harming living things; from deceit, stealing, unchastity, and from acquisitiveness.
2. Observance of self-disciplinary rules, cleanliness, calm, mortification, study and prayer.
3. Sitting in the proper postures for example, with the right foot upon the left thigh, the left foot upon the right thigh, the hands crossed, and the eyes focused on the tip of the nose.
4. Regulation of the breath: where the aim is to reduce the whole of being alive to one or two simple and rhythmic processes, all the muscles, voluntary and involuntary, and the nerve-currents, being brought under control.
5. Withdrawal of the senses from all sense objects, much as a tortoise retreats under his shell by drawing in its head and limbs. This step shuts out the outside world.
6. Concentration during which the mind is held steadily to the contemplation of a single idea or object until it is emptied of all else.
7. Meditation, a half unconscious condition affording a transition to the last step.

8. Samadhi, a trance in which the mind, now emptied of all content and no longer aware of either object or subject, is absorbed into the ultimate, and is one with it.

3. *The Vedanta System*

This system derives its name from the source of its leading doctrines, the Upanishads. The Vedanta system is the first attempt to set forth the monistic teachings of the Upanishads in a philosophic system. This system was prepared by Badarayana, a noted teacher who lived during the first century before the Christian era.

There are three gods which the Hindus worship:

1. Brahma is the creator and the least widely worshiped. Only half a dozen temples are dedicated to him. He is depicted in art as a kingly personage with four heads, reading the Vedas and riding on a white wild goose.

2. Shiva is the great god of the Hindus. He is known as the destroyer, the bringer of disease and death. His presence is felt at the funeral pyre. He is not purely evil as he has constructive and helpful aspects. He was originally the god of the mountain who caused destructive and punitive raids on the plains. He also grew medicinal herbs for the healing of man. He destroyed only to make room for new creations. He became identified with the process of reproduction in every realm of life – vegetable, animal and human. Shiva is also the patron saint of the ascetics and holy men. He is often represented as being in deep meditation with his naked body smeared with ashes and his hair braided after the fashion of an ascetic.

3. Vishnu is called the preserver. He is always benevolent. He watches from the skies and whenever he sees values threatened or good in peril, he exerts all his preservative influence in their behalf. He is usually represented with four arms, two hands holding symbols of his royal power (the mace and discus), and in his other two hands he has the emblems of his magic power and stainless purity (the conch and the lotus respectively). His head is surmounted by a high crown and diadem, his feet are blue, his vesture yellow, and his eyes lotus. Greatly admired by the Hindus, he is usually pictured as reclining or resting on the world serpent, Sheba or Ananta. His vehicle is the bird, Garuda. His symbol is the fish. His spouse is the lovely goddess of fortune and beauty, Lakshmi.

The Ganges River is the holy river to the Hindus. A popular myth explains that it issues from the feet of Vishnu in heaven and falls far below upon Shiva's head and flows out of his hair. A pilgrim center is located at the place where it issues strong and clear from the Himalayan mountains. Allahabad is a city which attracts millions of pilgrims to its melas or religious fairs. Benares is a holy city where most of the pilgrims go to attempt to wash away their sins.

Hinduism is paradoxically both one of the most liberal and one of the most conservative of religions. Liberalism flows from the intellectual freedom granted to its adherents – freedom whereby they may even deny the inspiration of the Vedas, the holiness of the Brahmins, the caste system – yet they remain Hindus provided they do not break the completely accepted moral practices of their localities, especially the dietary restrictions which prohibit inter-dining of the castes, taking a cup of water from one of a lower caste and the rigid marriage laws of the castes.

Nearly all Hindus accept the doctrines of the transmigration of souls and Nirvana.

1. *Transmigration of Souls*

The transmigration of souls or reincarnation has been held by primitives and people of higher cultural levels for centuries. It made its first appearance as a definite religious doctrine in the Upanishads.

The Hindus believe that at death the soul is reborn. The re-birth may be higher or lower than the previous birth, depending upon the conduct of the Hindu. He may be reborn into any of the forms of life: vegetable, animal or human.

The Law of Karma determines the rebirth of the soul. Karma means "deeds" or "works" and is the law that one's thoughts, words and deeds determine one's lot in future existences.

The rebirths of the soul are endless and each Hindu has the hope of being born, if in human form, in a higher caste.

2. *Nirvana*

The reaching of Nirvana is the ultimate goal of every Hindu. After a series of rebirths, often taking thousands of years, the soul is ready to enter Nirvana. The word Nirvana means "a blowing out" and is similar to the Christian's heaven.

BUDDHISM

CHAPTER 2

BUDDHISM

Buddhism was an attempt to reform Hinduism. It was founded in the sixth century B.C. by Siddhartha Gautama who is called The Buddha (The Enlightened One). He lived in the period of 563-483 B.C.

Buddhism was founded in India but has almost died out in the land of its birth. Today, there are more Buddhists in the United States than there are in India. It is found in Ceylon, Burma, Siam, Cambodia, Tibet, Japan and China.

The sacred books of Buddhism are the Tripitaka ("The Three Baskets of Wisdom"). The Tripitaka is divided into sermons, rules for the priesthood, and Buddhist doctrines. Many books have been added to the sacred literature of Buddhism.

It is claimed that there are 150,000,000 to 520,000,000 Buddhists, but many of them are also Confucianists or Taoists so they may be counted two or three times in a religious census.

King Suddhodhana Gautama lived in the Royal Palace in Kapilavista. He was wealthy but unhappy because he did not have a son to be his heir. He made many sacrifices to the gods in hopes of gaining a son. He studied the sacred literature of his people for many hours. When the king was fifty years old, Queen Maya gave birth to a son whom they called Siddhartha Gautama. People on horseback and elephants came from all over the country to congratulate the king and queen. Seven holy men came from the Himalayan mountains. They prophesied a great future for the child.

Prince Siddhartha was taught to manage elephants by an uncle. Another uncle taught him how to shoot straight with a bow and arrows. His father taught him how to train wild horses.

When the prince was twelve years old, a great celebration was arranged in the Royal Palace. At that time he put on the sacred thread which is a sort of confirmation of the Hindus. He took a vow to become an earnest student of the Holy Books of his father's religion.

Siddhartha was sent to the best known and most learned priests in the Sakya Kingdom to receive an education. The children of high caste studied literature, grammar, mathematics, astronomy and other subjects, but most of their time was devoted to the study of religion. The prince had to learn a new language, for all the sacred books were written in Sanskrit. At sixteen, Prince Siddhartha was as learned in Hinduism as any man in the Sikya Kingdom.

The same day as Prince Siddhartha was born, his future wife, Princess Yosodhara, was born. They were married when they were sixteen.

King Suddhodhana gave his son and daughter-in-law three beautiful castles with many servants where they lived a happy married life for ten years.

Prince Siddhartha knew little of life and people. He had been sheltered from the outside world. One day he saw sick people, old people, and a funeral procession in the market place. He had lived in palaces and studied many learned books for thirty years but this was his first experience with sickness, old age and death.

There must be something wrong with life to have illness, old age and death in it, he reasoned. He had never studied in any sacred book an explanation of how suffering was created. Now he wondered why all the people of his country were not as happy as his family.

The prince began to realize how wretched were the lives of many people in his country. He revolted against the caste system. The holy scriptures of Hinduism seemed wrong to him. He started visiting the market places to observe the poor wretched lives.

He left home and became a beggar-monk. His father was shocked. Princess Yosodhara had given birth to a son and it was thought that this would settle the restlessness in the prince's life. The prince knew that he would have to leave before he became attached to his son, so he left home at night while his wife and son were asleep. He shaved his head and beard and changed clothes with a beggar.

The night that the prince left home at the age of thirty is known as the Blessed Night of the Great Renunciation.

The prince wandered for seven years in search of wisdom. By his gentle voice and simple and wise conversation, he had a profound influence on all whom he met.

Bimbisara, the king of Mogadah, heard the prince speak with wisdom and offered him the position of chief advisor. This he refused.

The prince contacted the great teacher Alara who told him to study the Vedas in order to gain wisdom. Another great teacher Udaka told him the same thing. He had studied the Vedas for years but had never found an explanation of illness, old age, or death.

The prince then met some monks who told him that in order to gain wisdom he would have to torture and starve his body. The soul would become improved as the body suffered. He went into the forest where he starved his body until he was as thin as a skeleton. When he fainted, he abandoned this method of obtaining wisdom. Beginning to eat and drink again, he slowly regained his strength and began to think more clearly. He wandered day after day, living on berries and fruit, which he found in the woods, and on rice which was given him by the townspeople.

The prince became homesick for his wife and son but he knew that he would never be happy in the palace until he had gained the wisdom for which he sought.

When he became weary, he sat down to rest under a tree and made a vow that he would remain there until he realized his ambition of gaining wisdom. At last he claimed that he had found the first law of life — that from good must come good and from evil must come evil. This was one of the main laws of Hinduism but had not possessed the thinking of the prince.

The name of the prince now became Buddha, which means "The Enlightened One." The night that Buddha received his revelation is known as The Sacred Night. The tree under which Buddha sat is known as the Bo tree or The Tree of Wisdom. He remained under the Bo tree for forty-nine days meditating on the wisdom which he had acquired.

Buddha returned to Benares to seek several monks whom he had met who were also seeking the truth. He reasoned that it would be easier to teach those who were desirous of learning. Buddha began to question the holiness of the Vedas. This no one had ever done before.

He delivered a sermon to the monks in Benares which has become known as The Sermon of Benares in which he outlined the teachings of his new system.

He preached: "Water always flows downhill. Fire is always hot. Ice is always cold. Praying to all the gods in India will not make water flow uphill or fire cold or ice hot. That is because there are laws in life that make these things as they are. Prayers and sacrifices to the gods must therefore be useless. If that is true, then all the images representing the many gods are useless. If these gods have no power to change anything in the world, they should not be prayed to and worshiped. If a man does good, the results will be good, and if he does evil, the results will be evil, and all the gods in India cannot change that. Now, if that is really true, it must follow as the day follows night, that the Vedas, which tell people how to pray and how to sacrifice, are not holy. Our priests say to you that the Vedas and every word in them are holy. But I say to you that the Vedas are not sacred books. The Vedas teach us to believe that Brahma created people in castes. But that is not true to the First Law of Life. People are only divided into good people and bad people. They who are good, are good: and they who are bad, are bad. And it does not make any difference in what family they are born. I do not believe that Brahma created anything. The world was not created by Brahma.

"I believe that the world is going to exist forever and forever. It will never come to an end. And anything that has no end, has no beginning. The world was not created by anyone. The world always was.

"There are two extremes to keep away from. One is a life of pleasure; that is selfish and ignoble. The other is a life of self-torture; and that, too, is unworthy. For these two roads do not lead to the Good Life.

"The Eight-fold path teaches the Eight Rules of Life.

"Right Belief, which is the belief that truth is the guide of man;

"Right Resolve, to be calm all the time and never to do harm to any living creature;

"Right Speech, never to lie, never to slander anyone, and never to use coarse or harsh language;

"Right Behavior, never to steal, never to kill, and never to do anything that one may later regret or be ashamed of;

"Right Occupation, never to choose an occupation that is bad, like forgery, the handling of stolen goods, usury, and the like;

"Right Effort, always to strive after that which is good, and alway to keep away from that which is evil;

"Right Contemplation, always to be calm and not allow one's thoughts to be mastered by either joy or sorrow;

"Right Concentration is then found when all the other rules have been followed and one has reached the stage of perfect peace.

"The Five Commands of Uprightness are: Do not kill; Do not steal; Do not lie; Do not commit adultery; and Do not become intoxicated at any time."

Buddha gained the five monks in Benares as followers and

Buddhism was established. Buddha organized the monks into a Brotherhood of Monks. They became the preachers and teachers of Buddhism.

Buddha kept his promise to King Bimbisara of Mogadah. The king was converted from Hinduism to Buddhism. Buddhism grew and gained thousands of followers. His fame soon reached his homeland.

Buddha's father sent a message to Buddha to return home. He returned home and presented his teachings to his family. His son was converted. Princess Yosodhara was made the first nun of the Holy Order of Buddha. The land of Sakjas accepted his teachings.

Buddha's cousin, Decadattha, professed to follow him but was jealous of his fame and plotted against him. Decadattha tried to betray Buddha to the kings of the countries through which he traveled, but his plot failed.

Buddha died at the age of 80 in 483 B.C.

The writings of Buddha were collected after his death into three collections called the *Tripitaka* (Three Baskets of Wisdom) which became the sacred scriptures of Buddhism.

The Jatakas are stories of the various lives which Buddha was supposed to have lived during his reincarnations. He was claimed to have had 530 reincarnations: 42 times a god; 85 times a king; 24 times a prince; 22 times a learned man; 2 times a thief; 1 time a slave; 1 time a gambler. Many times a lion, a deer, a horse, an eagle, a bull, a snake and even a frog. After Buddha became the enlightened one, he was no longer born again but he entered Nirvana.

Buddhism was the first missionary religion. Whereas Hinduism did not accept converts, Buddhism accepted all who would follow the eightfold path.

Soon after Buddha's death, his followers disagreed as to his meanings and many sects were formed within Buddhism. Buddha preached against images and idol worshiping but his followers soon set up his image in many temples and made Buddha himself an idol.

The four elementary truths of Buddhism are:

1. Both birth and death bring grief, and life is vain.
2. The cause of grief, and hence of vanity of life, is the indulgences of desire.
3. With the ending of desire will come surcease from grief.
4. The best way to end desire is by application of wisdom and intelligence to life.

The five great obstacles to the higher life are: sloth, pride, malice, lust and doubt.

Buddhism does not admit that man has a soul as it appeals to man to be his own reformer, ruler and judge. Buddhism gives no authoritative account of creation. There is no explanation of how death or sin entered the world. There is no promise of divine assistance nor of remission of sin.

The Ten Commandments of Buddhism are:

1. Thou shalt not kill any living being.
2. Thou shalt not take that which is not thine.
3. Thou shalt not commit adultery.
4. Thou shalt not prevaricate, but shall speak the word of truth.
5. Thou shalt not partake of intoxicating liquors.
6. Thou shalt not partake of food after midday.
7. Thou shalt not be present at any dramatic, dancing, or musical performance.
8. Thou shalt not use any personal adornment or any perfume.
9. Thou shalt not sleep on a broad, comfortable bed.
10. Thou shalt not be owner of any gold or silver.

Buddhism is divided into two major groups: the Hinayana – retiring from the world to seek enlightenment for oneself; and the Mahayana – remaining in the world to enlighten oneself and others.

Meditation plays a great part in the practice of Buddhism. There are several rules to govern the practice of meditation.

The ten requirements for the place of meditation are:

1. For beginners the place should be clean and quiet.
2. Its temperature should be comfortable during all seasons.
3. It should be well ventilated.
4. Beginners should not meditate when the weather is either too warm or too cold.
5. The place should be neither too dark nor too light.
6. It should not offer any view that distracts the mind.
7. Beginners in meditation should avoid association with men of fame or with those who like to argue.
8. Beginners in meditation should avoid association with those who like competitive games.
9. Beginners in meditation should avoid all places of danger such as fire, flood, storm and the haunts of criminals.
10. Beginners should not meditate by the sea nor in the vicinity of pleasure resorts.

The ten rules of physical condition for meditation are:

1. Your stomach should be neither empty nor full.
2. Dress comfortably in clean clothes, but never be greedy for fine clothing.
3. Regulate your hours for sleep.
4. Keep your leisure hours for meditation.
5. Do not waste time writing poems or essays on Zen.
6. Do not meditate immediately after meals.
7. Do not try to meditate when you are too nervous.
8. If possible, remove the shoes while meditating.
9. Bathe daily.
10. A healthy body means healthy meditation. First of all, take care of your health.

There are ten things which must be known about the mind in relation to meditation:

1. Do not think of either good or bad nor of right and wrong.
2. Do not think of either the past or the future.
3. Do not be ambitious to attain realization. Do not desire to become a Buddha.
4. Both before and after meditation think of Anicca, impermanency; think also of Anatta, the impossibility of identifying any self entity in either your mind or your body.
5. Do not cling to subjectivity; do not cling to objectivity. Non-thinking and non-clinging purify the mind.
6. Before and after meditation repeat your vow to save all sentient beings.
7. When your mind wanders, clasp your hands tightly, or concentrate upon the tip of your nose. Usually awareness of the lower part of your abdomen prevents mind wandering.
8. If you feel dizzy during meditation, concentrate your mind upon your forehead.
9. If you feel sick, concentrate your mind upon your toes.
10. Without moving or holding anything in your mind, or clinging either to a positive or negative idea, advance step by step ahead in your meditation until you hear the sound of one hand.

Buddhism accepts the Hindu theory of transmigration of souls. It discounts the authority of the old Vedic laws and discards completely the doctrines of caste and the priesthood of Hinduism. Buddhism stresses moral living much more than ritualism. Buddhism stresses salvation for the masses rather than for the individual. Buddhism has no room for a personal god, priests, prayers, temples or ritual in its teachings, but in practice Buddhists have built temples and employ a ritual in worship.

Buddhism has adapted itself to the country in which it is located. In China, it has taken on the character of Taoism. In Japan, it was influenced by the national religion of Shintoism. Christianity made its impact upon Buddhism. It has withered and died in India, its birthplace, due to the persecution of Hinduism and the invading forces of Mohammedanism.

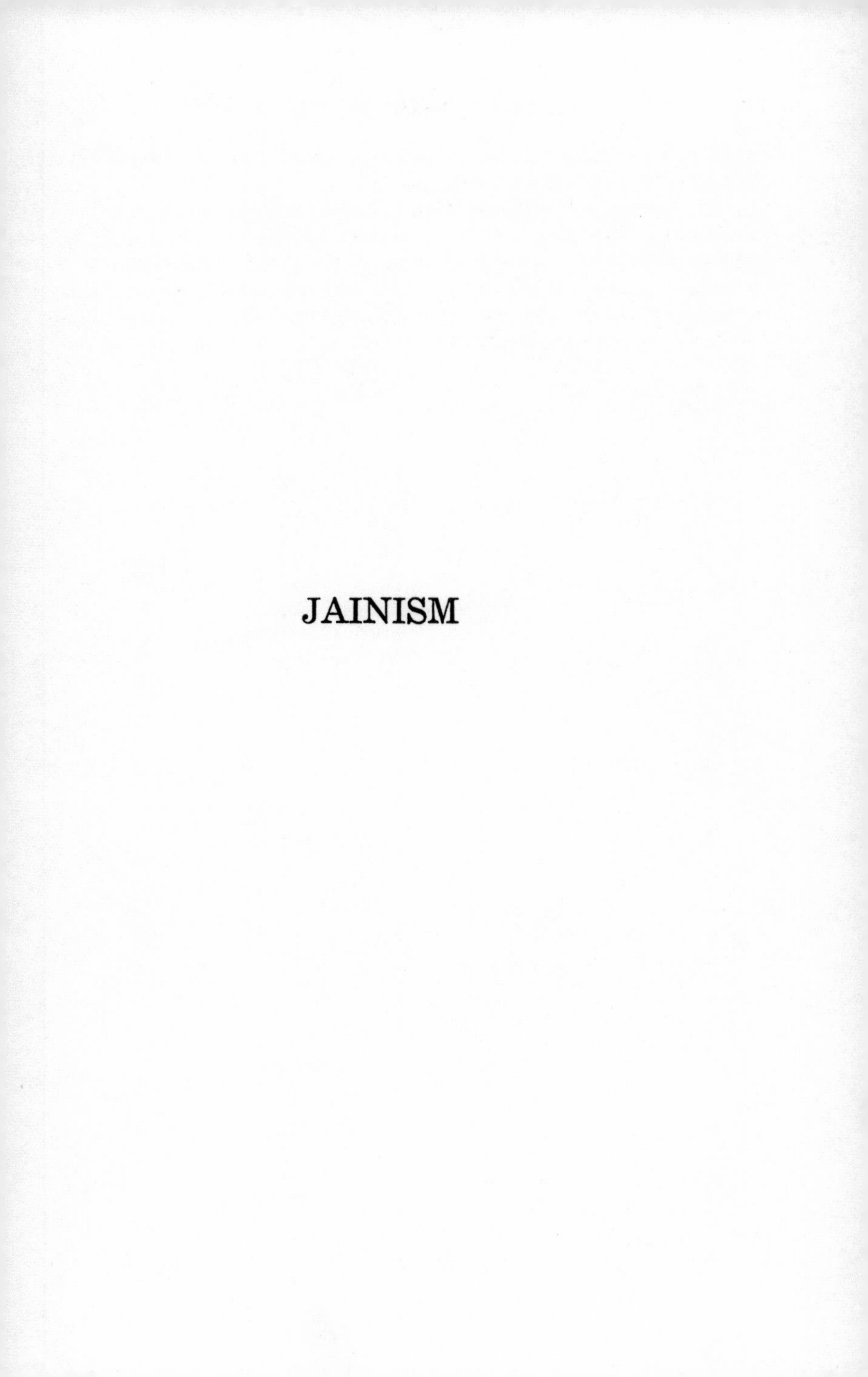

JAINISM

CHAPTER 3

JAINISM

Jainism was another reform movement within Hinduism. It was founded in the sixth century B.C. by Nataputta Vardhamara also called Prince Mahavira who lived in the period of 599-527 B.C. This religion was also founded in India.

The sacred books of Jainism are the Agamas which are the sermons of Prince Mahavira. The basic teachings of the Agamas are the reverence for life, vegetarianism, ascetism, the opposition to war and non-violence even in self-defense.

Jainism is found exclusively in India, especially in the cities of the central and southern part.

Jainism has been divided into two major groups: the Svetambara (white-robed)—the priests are always clad in white; and the Digambara (sky-clad) in which the priests wear nothing but a loin cloth. The differences in clothing is symbolic of their doctrinal differences.

The stories of the lives of Buddha and Prince Mahavira are so similar that the question has arisen as to whether these religious leaders were the same man or two different persons. It is the belief of this author that they were two different people. Mahavira was older than Buddha and died before Buddha, although he lived a great deal of his life during the time of Buddha.

In 600 B.C. the people of the Kingdom of Mogadah gathered in the capital for a great celebration. The streets were gaily lit, sacrifices were offered to the Hindu gods in the temples. Hymns were sung before Brahma, the creator, and Vishnu, the preserver. King Sneyana distributed alms among the poor. The prisoners were set free.

This was not a religious or a military celebration but was held to celebrate the birth of a prince, Vardhamara. The Holy Men came from the Ganges River and the Himalayan Mountains to see the prince.

The prince was taught to use the bow and arrows, manage wild horses and elephants and was given the name of Mahavira (the

Great Hero) when a mad elephant bull charged Vardhamara and his playmates. Vardhamara grabbed the elephant's trunk, climbed upon his head and rode him back to the stable.

Vardhamara put on the sacred thread of Hinduism when he was twelve years old. He took a vow of allegiance to the religion of his father and was sent to the priests to study Hinduism.

Prince Mahavira liked to study but he disliked his teachers. He did not like the vain attitude of the priests' teaching that they were better than the other castes.

Prince Mahavira married Princess Yosadha when he was nineteen years old and they lived in the royal palace of the Kingdom of Mogadah for ten years.

Both parents of Prince Mahavira deliberately starved themselves to death when he was twenty-eight years old. Death by starvation was considered a holy death by the people of India. The prince deeply mourned the death of his parents. His older brother was now King of Mogadah.

The prince mourned the death of his parents for two years and then left home to go to the city of Vesali where he changed clothes with a beggar-monk. He took a vow of silence and vowed to remain silent for twelve years.

Prince Mahavira begged food and lived on wild berries and fruit. He remained silent for twelve years and meditated upon the teachings of Hinduism. He saw many things in Hinduism with which he could not agree and thought of the ways of changing and improving the teachings of his people.

After his twelve years of silence, he started preaching. He organized a brotherhood of monks and a sisterhood of nuns.

Mahavira preached:

"All of a man's life is suffering. Birth is suffering; illness is suffering; death is suffering; not getting what you want is suffering.

"All of the suffering of the world comes from desire. People suffer and are unhappy because they want so many things. No matter how much a man gets of food, wealth and fame, he always wants more. Desire then is the cause of all suffering.

"Suffering can be overcome when desire is overcome. When a man gives up all desires, then he can prepare himself for the greatest happiness of the soul, which is Nirvana.

"The way to Nirvana is through the Three Jewels of the Soul which are Right Conviction, Right Knowledge and Right Conduct.

"Right Conduct comes first and the right conduct of a man is found in the Five Commandments of the soul:

"Do not kill any living thing, or hurt any living thing by word, thought or deed;

"Do not steal;

"Do not lie;

"Do not live an unchaste life and never become intoxicated;

"Do not covet or desire anything.

"We cannot believe in castes and we know that prayers do not have any value or do anyone any good. It is not in prayer, nor in sacrifice, nor in idol-worship that you find forgiveness and the way to the good life. Only by doing good can you reach Nirvana. Within yourselves lies salvation!"

Mahavira taught that even trees, water, fire, and certain vegetables have souls. If a man lived a bad life, he might not only be born again as an animal but even as a vegetable.

He taught that there were seven hells under the earth, one below the other, each more terrible. Bad souls who kept on being bad would find themselves in the hells according to their badness.

Mahavira taught that a soul has weight and if a soul sins, it becomes heavy and sinks down. If a soul is good and pure, it rises and floats up to one of the twenty-six heavens which rise one above another. The twenty-sixth heaven is Nirvana.

Mahavira traveled through India for thirty years preaching against the caste system and explaining his beliefs concerning heaven and hell.

The prince took ill at Pava when he was seventy years old. He called his followers together and preached his last sermon:

"Of all my teachings, the First of my Five Commandments is the most important.

"Do not kill any living thing, or hurt any living thing by word, thought or deed.

"Do not kill animals for food. Do not hunt nor fish, nor even kill the least creature at any time. Do not kill the mosquito that bites you or the bee that stings you. Do not go to war. Do not fight back at your attacker. Do not step upon a worm on the road side. Even the worm has a soul."

The First Commandment of non-injury to anything that has a soul is called Ahimsa. Jainism is pluralistic and groups all things into two categories: lifeless things called Ajiva and living things called Jiva.

Jains believe that Jainism was founded by 24 Jinas (conquerors) and that Mahavira was one of these Jinas and was not the only founder.

The Jains are not permitted to till the soil for fear of killing a worm. They are not permitted to cut down trees. They are not permitted to boil water for fear of killing invisible insects. They are not permitted to use furnaces for fear of burning flies and insects. Nearly all the Jains have become merchants, traders, and bankers as they could not become farmers, soldiers and still remain true to their religion. Many have become very wealthy.

There are 40,000 Jain temples in India and the temple on Mt. Abu is one of the seven wonders of India. The sect maintains homes for cows and hospitals for sick animals with wards for sick birds and insects. The Jains are very charitable as their religion is a vital part of their lives.

Buddha and Mahavira were both Hindu princes. They were both brave boys, both earnestly studied their religion, both were happily married, both left their homes to become beggar-monks, both found faults with many of the teachings of their religion and both thought and meditated for years before preaching their teachings to the people. Both followed the Hindu doctrines of Karma, reincarnation and Nirvana, and both rejected the Hindu teachings of the Holiness of Castes, salvation by prayer and sacrifices, and the absolute truth of the Vedas. They both believed that one should not depend upon the help of God but live according to Right Conviction and Right Knowledge. But they disagreed on what is the right conduct of good men.

Buddha taught the middle road of moderation and that all extremes are evil while Mahavira taught the road of self-torture called Ascetism and that self-denial and torture help man to reach the good life.

The early followers of Mahavira did not have any temples because they did not believe in prayer and in gods. Later they built temples and made stone images of Mahavira. In time these images became objects of worship.

Mahavira formulated the vows which are required of the monks and laymen of Jainism.

The five vows of the monks are:

1. Renounce all killing of living things, movable or immovable.
2. Renounce all sins of lying speech arising from anger, greed, fear or mirth.
3. Renounce all taking of anything not given.
4. Renounce all sexual pleasures.

5. Renounce all attachments – whether too little or much, small or great, living or lifeless things.

The twelve vows of laymen are:

1. Never intentionally to take life of a sentient creature (hence, never to till the soil, nor engage in butchering, fishing, brewing, or any occupation involving the taking of life).
2. Never to lie.
3. Never to steal.
4. Never to be unchaste.
5. To check greed, by placing a limit upon one's wealth and giving away any excess.
6. To avoid temptation to sin by, for example, refraining from unnecessary travel.
7. To limit the number of things in daily use.
8. To be on guard against evils that can be avoided.
9. To keep stated periods of meditation.
10. To observe special periods of self-denial.
11. To spend occasional days as a monk.
12. To give alms, especially in support of ascetics.

The monks preached:

"When the Lord Mahavira preached, not only did all human beings understand him, but even the creatures that crawl, and the birds that fly and the souls of the vegetables and the trees, all these understood him. And they understood him because he preached a religion for all things that have souls, a religion which is a blessing to all creatures of the world."

They continued:

"When Mahavira walked, he carried a soft broom to use in sweeping the path whenever it might be covered with insects. Out of doors he cleared the ground before lying down to rest or sleep and he examined his bed to be sure that it was free from eggs and living beings. He refused all raw food of any kind and took only food into his begging bowl prepared originally for someone else and left over. He carried a cloth for straining water before drinking it. He always went carefully through a bowl of food to see if any of it was affected by eggs, sprouts, worms, mildew, cobwebs or any living thing."

Jainism could not become a universal religion because no one could grow fruit or vegetables and the people would die of hunger, thirst and cold if they all became Jains. A missionary movement has started among the Jains in recent years. The group has published a large selection of pamphlets and booklets of a propaganda nature in English. English magazines have published many articles stressing the Jain's doctrine of non-violence.

The Jain's doctrine of not killing any living thing has accounted for much of the diseases of India. It is a fact that animals and insects are the carriers of germs which cause disease. Malaria is spread by mosquitoes while Cholera and Bubonic Plagues are spread by lice who live on rats. The Jains by not killing the insects which spread disease are instrumental in spreading these diseases and many epidemics have taken a large toll of lives in India.

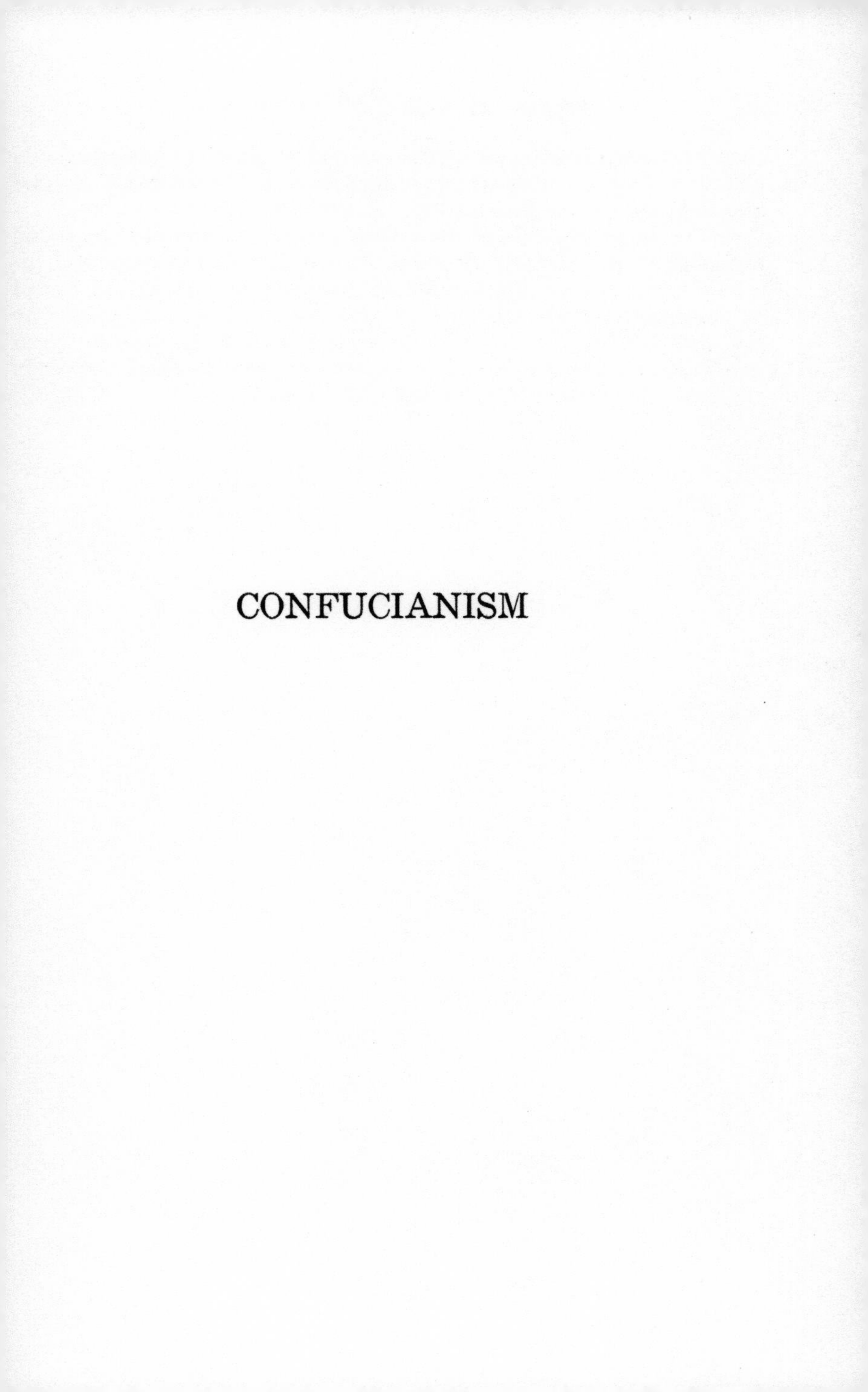

CONFUCIANISM

Chapter 4

CONFUCIANISM

Confucianism was founded in the sixth century B.C. by Ch'in K'ung who is known in the West by the Latinized form of Confucius. He lived in the period of 551-479 B.C. China was the birthplace of Confucianism. The sacred books of Confucianism are The Analects and the Five Kings.

There are from 300 to 400 million Confucians, although many are also Buddhists and Taoists. There are no sects in Confucianism, as its followers are free to join any other faith.

Shuh-liang Heih, the father of Confucius, was an unhappy man. He had nine daughters but no son. He desired a son who would worship his spirit after his death.

Shuh-liang Heih, Governor of Tsow, died three years after the birth of his son and left his family in poor financial circumstances. The mother managed to give her son a good education. Confucius was praised by his teachers as he understood many things which grown people were incapable of understanding.

People came for miles to talk to young Confucius because of his wisdom. He was married at nineteen and given the position of Keeper of the Granaries. He made many improvements and was promoted to The Superintendent of Fields. His wife gave birth to a son and two daughters.

Confucius spent his leisure hours in studying history, music and poetry and his knowledge increased daily. His home became the meeting place of all the learned men of his district. Men of all ages came to Confucius to ask questions. He was always glad to teach whatever he knew to those willing to learn.

Students flocked to him from all over China as his fame spread. He established a school, not of boys to be taught the elements of learning, but of young and inquiring minds who wished to be instructed in the principles of right conduct and government. He accepted the aid of his students but did not deny admittance to any who could not pay. By the age of thirty-four, he had 3,000 students.

When Confucius was fifty-two years old he became the Chief Magistrate (mayor) of Chung-tu. He made many improvements, and the people were happier than ever before. He rewarded those who were good and he punished those who were bad.

Confucius became the minister of crime for the entire province of Lu. He began a study of prisons and the kind of people who filled them. He came to the conclusion that prisoners were of the poor and uneducated classes and so began an educational reform movement to eliminate poverty and ignorance. He taught the people useful trades and occupations to enable them to earn a living. He pleaded for good rulers who would inspire the people and set a good example for them. After two years under Confucius' rule as minister of crime, all the prisons and courts were empty.

Confucius' advice was sought by the new Duke of Lu (C Ting) and Lu became one of the richest and strongest provinces in the entire Empire of China. Other rulers became jealous and devised a plot to keep Ting from listening to the advice of Confucius. They sent the duke gifts of dancing girls and racehorses. He began to spend all his time at the race tracks. Confucius realized that the government was being neglected, but since the Duke was gone all the time, Confucius couldn't lead and advise him. Lu became poor and the prisons were filled with criminals. Confucius left the province, grieved and saddened.

For fifteen years Confucius and his followers wandered in search of a wise ruler but they failed to find one. Confucius' wife died and he returned to Lu where he was asked to become the chief advisor to the Duke. He spent the remainder of his life writing the history of Lu, gathering a collection of old Chinese poetry. He hoped that his books would spread his ideals and teachings throughout China.

As he esteemed knowledge to be the greatest good in the world, Confucius liked to discuss the importance of education. The thought of the poverty and misery throughout China saddened him.

He was greatly disappointed in his son, Li, who disliked to study. Li's son, Kleigh, was like his grandfather and lived and studied with Confucius.

Confucius died in 487 B.C. and his death was mourned throughout China. Many students built shelters near his burial place and studied his teachings during the three-year period of mourning.

Kleigh set to work to collect the sayings and lessons which he had learned from his grandfather. He taught in order to live while working on the book, "The Doctrine of the Middle-path."

A hundred years after the death of Confucius, a child was born in Lu named Mang. He grew up and taught against the selfish and unjust princes and ministers. He taught the wisdom of Confucius which he named Confucianism after its founder.

His pupils called Mang, Mang-tze which means, Mang the Philosopher. He has become known as Mencius.

Two hundred and fifty years after Confucius, the Emperor in Shih Hwang-ti tried to erase the memory and teachings of Confucius from China. He burned all the available books of Confucius, Kleigh and Mencius, which were written on bamboo.

In 212 B.C. some of the officers who loved the books of the masters stole them and walled them into the buildings so they couldn't be burned. The emperor then ordered all the scholars who had memorized the writings of the masters to be killed and five hundred scholars were killed. Hundreds were driven from China and many were put to work on the Great Wall of China which was being built. The emperor died and the people took out the books which had been buried. A celebration in honor of Confucius was held.

Confucius had little faith in the gods. There is nothing in his teachings which indicate any reliance whatever upon the gods for achieving salvation.

In 1 A.D. the gradual process of raising Confucius to his present place of eminence began. He was canonized as Duke Ni. In 57 A.D. regular sacrifices to Confucius were ordered at all imperial and provincial colleges. In 89 A.D., he was raised to the rank of Earl. In 267 A.D., more elaborate sacrifices to Confucius were ordered to be observed four times a year. In 555 A.D., separate temples for the worship of Confucius were decreed for every provincial capitol. In 740 A.D. the image was moved from the side to the center of the Imperial College to stand with the historic kings of China. In 1068 A.D. he was raised to the full rank of Emperor. In 1907 the Empress Dowager raised Confucius to the first grade of worship – ranking him with the deities of Heaven and Earth.

Confucius, who in life was beaten and hounded, is now a god for all China. He had no sheltering place in life, but now has over 1500 temples to house his tablets. He was starved but now has over 62,000 animals offered to his ghost every year. He who did not believe in prayer has been made the object of prayer. He who had little regard for the gods has been made co-equal with heaven.

The basic teachings of Confucianism may be summarized:

1. Human nature is good; evil is essentially unnatural.

2. The human will is completely free, and the conduct of man is not predetermined. He is master of his own choices.

3. Virtue is its own reward. Human conduct is not religiously conditioned. One does not do good for reward or refrain from evil for fear of punishment.

4. Confucius' system offers no outside help from the gods or anyone else. It is a self-effort system. He taught the Golden Rule, though expressed in negative form, sometimes called the Silver Rule: "What you do not want others to do unto you, do not do unto them."

The family is the basic unit of Chinese society. Confucius taught that each family ought to be like a little government. Parents should take care of their children and give them a good education. Children should respect and obey their parents and do all they can to make them happy.

The Chinese have a tremendous sense of family solidarity and this is expressed in what is called Ancestor Worship. The family group includes the dead as well as the living. In each home is the ancestral shrine, which is usually found in a small niche specially built for it. It contains the tablets on which are written the names of the departed. Families are grouped in clans. Ancestral halls are built for the use of the whole clan, whose members have the same name. These halls contain a roll of the members. Important clan festivals are held in these halls and the spirits of the dead are invoked for protection and help. Fortune and misfortune are controlled by these spirits. There is a family pilgrimage in spring and autumn to the graves of ancestors which are buried together in the clan cemetery.

The Analects is a collection of the sayings of Confucius and some of his disciples.

The Yi-ching or Book of Changes is a very difficult and obscure book of divination which Confucius re-arranged and commented upon.

The Shu-ching or Book of History is concerned with the Sage Kings of the Golden Age.

The Shi-ching or Book of Odes consists of ballads and songs.

The Ch'un Ch'iu is a record of events in the reigns of the rulers of the province of Lu.

The Li Chi or Book of Rites is a collection of treatises on ceremonies.

The Great Learning was originally chapter 39 of the Li Chi and seems to be more dependent for its point of view on Hsiim-tze (298-238 A.D.) rather than on Confucius. It was initially designed to serve as the basis of the education of gentlemen in general, princes in particular. It was the first text studied by boys in classical Chinese.

The Doctrine of the Mean was originally chapter 28 of Li Chi. It is an excellent exposition of the philosophical presuppositions of Confucian thought, dealing particularly with the relation of human nature to the underlying moral order of the universe.

The Book of Mencius was written in the third century B.C. and is a collection of the writings and sayings of Mencius. It constitutes the first attempt to reach a sound and systematic exposition of Confucius' philosophy.

The ethical thought of Confucius sprang from a double realization: (1) that the China of his day was disturbingly corrupt, and (2) the moral condition of the country was not beyond redemption. The situation was bad but was not hopeless. Man's practices had grown corrupt but man himself had not become completely corrupt. He was still as apt to be good as to be evil.

The word *li* was one of the most important words used by Confucius in formulating his program for the recovery of China. It is difficult to translate. Many meanings have been given to *li:* "propriety"; "courtesy"; "reverence"; "rites and ceremonies"; "the correct forms of social ceremony"; "ritual"; "ritual and music"; "the due order of public ceremony"; "the ideal standard of social and religion conduct"; "the religious and moral way of life."

There are five great relationships in the ethical teaching of Confucius.

1. Kindness in the father, filial piety in the son.
2. Gentility in the eldest brother, humility and respect in the younger.
3. Righteous behavior in the husband, obedience in the wife.
4. Human consideration in elders, deference in juniors.
5. Benevolence in rulers, loyalty in ministers and subjects.

If these ten attitudes are attained, then the highest propriety (*li*) will be actualized, perfect harmony will reign.

Confucius was equally emphatic about the importance of the relationship between the rulers and their subjects. If the rulers would adopt and act upon the highest principles and laws of social propriety, then the spiritual climate of the whole state would be changed. Then all subjects, high and low, would be led to live more virtuously.

Confucius stated that people were at heart good and responsive to good in those above them, to whom they looked for leadership. "If a country had none but good rulers for a hundred years, crime would be stamped out and the death penalty abolished."

Several schools of thought arose to challenge the teachings of

Confucius. They each proposed a different approach to the moral and political problems of the times.

1. Taoists were not gentle with the Confucianists. They were bitter toward all advocates of social discipline or managed economy.

2. The Mohists founded by Mo-tze or Mo-ti (468-390 B.C.) thought that the government should operate strictly under religious sanctions and always insisted on simplicity and thrift everywhere. Its founder wanted to do away with all the Chou institutions and build up a community of workers generally alike in station and filled with homely goodwill and brotherly kindness toward each other and all men. Mo-tze was motivated by two major aims: (1) to unite all his followers in a working brotherhood altruistically devoted to the common good, and (2) to have all men do the will of Heaven and the spirits.

3. The Legalists were a loosely associated group composed of thinkers with a wide variety of views. They all agreed that the disjointed and easy-going feudal system must give place to a social order held together by a tough all-embracing law in all the states. Many laid down rules which anticipated present-day totalitarianism, while others held the position which made and repealed laws and alliances according to expediency and immediate advantage.

4. Mencius was the orthodox champion of Confucianism. He magnified and gave studied emphasis to Confucius' belief in the innate goodness of man and the adequacy of the feudal system to develop and maintain that goodness. He believed wholeheartedly in the innate goodness of human nature. Realizing that war destroyed the possibility of attaining his ideals of government, he constantly preached against it. His religious views were types of mysticism as he believed in a guiding will from heaven. He believed that within each person there is a "vast-flowing vital energy."

5. Hsiin Tzu was the heterodox champion of Confucianism. He had a great immediate following and influence. Rejecting two cardinal principles of Mencius: that man's nature is innately good and that heaven watches over earth with something of a personal concern, he believed that man by nature is bad and his goodness is only acquired training. He is capable under proper conditions of indefinite improvement. If left to himself, he grows crooked. Education of the right kind will help to subdue the bad in human nature and develop the good. He emphasized *li* – the ceremonies and rules of proper conduct.

TAOISM

CHAPTER 5

TAOISM

Taoism was founded in the sixth century B.C. by Lao-tze, who is called the Old Philosopher in China.

The sacred book of Taoism is Tao-Teh-King which is called The Book of Reason and Virtue. This is the shortest sacred book in the world, as it contains only 5,000 words. It is divided into two sections: the first section called Tao, the why of the universe; and the second section called Teh, the how of life.

Lao-tze was born in a small hamlet, Keorh-Jin, in the district of Tsow, China.

At an early age, Lao-tze became the Keeper of the Royal Archives in the city of Lo-Yang. This position gave Lao an opportunity for a great deal of study. He gained the respect and admiration of many people when he began to express his opinions on philosophy and religion.

The rulers became so selfish and dishonorable that Lao decided to leave the place where he had lived nearly all of his life, though he was now ninety years of age.

He went as far as the border of the province where he was recognized by the Guardian of the Border. The Guardian of the Border told him that he would have to write a book of his teachings before he could pass. He sat down and wrote Tao-Teh-King, which became the sacred book of Taoism. He was allowed to pass and was not heard of again.

The Tao-Teh-King is a small book which is packed full of thought-provoking statements. Some are easy to understand, some are hard to understand, and some are impossible to understand.

The definition of Tao is not given. It has been interpreted as The Way, the Path, Reason, Word, and God. Lao-tze stated that no one can understand Tao who does not already know all about it.

Lao-tze taught against killing people in war and against killing criminals, because he thought that people are not made any better and crime is not reduced because of capital punishment. The only way to make people good is by treating them with kindness.

Lao-tze was of an inquisitive, speculative, adventurous nature and he was always asking the question, why. He sought to find the reason for the cause of each action.

Taoism started as a philosophy and was developed into a religion during the Han dynasty around 200 B.C.

Many large books have been written attempting to explain Tao-Teh-King. The followers of Taoism began to study the explanations rather than the book and naturally many ideas of the interpreters were added.

The Taoists worship many idols. They worship dragons of every kind. They worship rats, weasels, and snakes. They believe that if they carry certain ashes, stones, or certain writings on them then bullets cannot kill them, water cannot drown them and fire cannot burn them. The belief in devils, demons, vampires, goblins and every other kind of evil spirit became common in Taoism.

China had a long history of spirit worship. The Chinese believed that all things in nature had spirits. They called the good spirits, Shen, and they called the evil spirits, Kiver. When Taoism came with its spirit worship, it was easy for the Chinese to accept it.

The three Jewels of Taoism are Compassion, Moderation, and Modesty.

Chuang-tai, one of the greatest thinkers of Taoism, wrote:

"It is all pervasive; it fills the universe with sublime grandeur; it causes the sun and moon to revolve in their orbits; it gives life to the most microscopic insect. In itself formless, it is the source of all form; inaudible, it is the source of all sound; invisible, it is the origin of all sight; inactive, it produces and sustains every phenomenon. It is impartial, impersonal, and passionless."

The Book of Recompense declares:

"Advance in all that is in harmony with good; retreat from all that is opposed to it. Walk not in the paths of depravity, nor deceive yourselves by sinning in the dark where none can see you. Accumulate virtue, and store up merit; treat all with love and gentleness; be loyal; be dutiful; be respectful to your elders and kind to your juniors; be upright yourselves in order that you may reform others; pity the orphan and the widow; reverence the aged, cherish the young; do not injure even insects, grass or trees. When a man gains his desires, let it be as though his good fortune were your own; when one suffers loss, as though you suffered it yourself. Never publish the failings of another, or make a parade of your own merits; put a stop to evil, and afford every encouragement to goodness. When you are reviled, cherish no resentment; be kind and generous without seeking any return."

The Taoist rejects all learning and scoffs at all hunger for education. He does not believe in gods and opposes all forms of worship, sacrifices and prayers as both vain and impertinent.

Chapter 4 of Chuang Tzu says:

"Unify your attention. Do not listen (to that perceived by) the ear, but listen (to that perceived by) the heart. Do not listen (to that perceived by) the heart, but listen (to that perceived by) the soul. That which you understand does not come by the ears, but by the heart. The spirit should then be empty and take hold of reality. The union with the Tao is not obtained except by emptiness. It is this emptiness which is the renewing of their heart."

The Tao is impartial and plays no favorites. The complete man is unselfish, selfless and without egoism.

The Tao is orderly as there are no collisions in the universe. The Chinese like to talk things over. They often settle local conflicts or prevent them with a feast.

The Tao is humble. All things depend upon it for their existence. Yet it does not desire the reputation of its meritorious work and does not assume the reputation of doing so. It loves and nourishes all beings and does not make itself the owner. It is always without desire. It may even be mentioned in small things.

The first effort of Taoism is to realize that the world does not limit the privileges of others where there is no interference with freedom. The Taoists live in walled towns and the officials and soldiers live on the taxes of the peasants. The rulers claimed that their positions were granted to them by the favor of heaven and they were chosen to rule the peasants.

The Taoists attacked the moral and legal restraints which were advocated by Confucius. They developed the ideal of the small state. They censured the materialism of their day. They looked with critical eyes at the luxurious customs of their day. They urged government frugality and light taxes.

They claimed that people go hungry due to the fact that the rulers waste taxes. People are difficult to rule due to the meddlesomeness of the rulers.

They wrote, "The more beautiful the palaces, the more barren and neglected the fields. To adorn oneself with beautiful garments, to carry sharp swords, to be glutted with food and drink, with treasures in abundance — this means robbing and begging. These have nothing to do with the Tao."

The Taoists stressed contentment. "There is no greater calamity than not to be contented. There is no greater evil than continually increasing desire. Therefore note, he who understands sufficiently to be content is continually content."

Taoism in modern China is divided into two schools. The Northern School emphasized meditation, metaphysical speculation and proper breathing. The Southern School, headed by the Taoist pope until 1927 at Lung Hu Shan, dispensed charms, amulets and incantations.

The emperor was the model for all men. Good rulers will have a peaceful, harmonious state. If the state is in disorder, it is evident that the ruler has lost his power of the Tao and heaven is displeased.

The Taoists have always been most prosperous in times of trouble and confusion.

The central consideration of Taoism has both a positive and a negative aspect. On the positive side, one must exhibit within himself the nature of the Tao and be characterized by its quietude of power, its production without possession, action without self-assertion, development without domination. On the negative side, one is not to meddle with the smooth course of nature going on her blessed way. It is possible to achieve without doing.

The attendant virtues in human life are kindness, sincerity, and humility. If one does not meddle with others, human relations will fall as the Tao brings them to pass and there will be a natural and simple spontaneous birth of true love, real kindness, simplicity and contentment in the lives and relationships of men.

There have been three periods in the development of Taoism:

1. The philosophical or formative phase, characterized by strong mystical interests.
2. The magical phase.
3. The phase of intermittent recognition by the Chinese government as the official religion of the empire.

Chuang-tzu, the most famous of philosophical Taoists except for Lao-tze, lived in the fourth century B.C. He popularized the teachings of Lao-tze. He wrote thirty-three essays which were brilliantly written, containing many anecdotes and entertaining allegory. He used imaginary conversation to enhance literary charm. He was true to Taoist teaching in giving Tao centrality. Chuang-Tzu likened the confusion of men to the puzzlement which would surely reign in the non-human world if creatures could make comparison of excellencies and defects. He went further than the Tao-Teh-Ching.

The Tao-Teh-Ching suggested that anyone who possessed the

secret of Tao became immune to the attack of armed men and wild animals as the one who is endued with ample virtue which Tao engenders may be compared to an infant whom no venomous reptile can sting. He who attains Tao attains everlasting life.

In the first century A.D., the magical emphasis in Taoism had become supreme. Chang-ling migrated from Eastern to Western China and founded a secret society which was dedicated primarily to alchemy and the cultivation of the Taoist meditative trance.

In the fourth century A.D. Ko Hung wrote a famous book on magical matters and spent the last years of his life on the Lo-fu mountain experimenting with a pill of immortality. He described in detail his breathing exercises, dietetics, alchemy and the magic of his time. The object of the breathing exercises was to increase the spiritual powers of the body and mind; the dietetics were to prolong life and particularly to enable one to live exclusively on air and dew. Immunity to sickness or death from old age could not be prevented by this method alone. The object of alchemy was to discover a liquid or eatable gold as a commodity which would confer immortality on those who would swallow it.

In 165 A.D. Emperor Huan of the second Han dynasty ordered official offerings to Lao-Tze and the building of temples in his honor.

In the seventh century A.D., Li-Shih-Min established the great T'ang dynasty which gave Taoism imperial recognition as an organized religion.

Taoism's reconstruction of the Chinese religion was not sincere. There were instances of outright fabrication. The Emperor Chen T'sung of the Sung dynasty effected by fraud the final step in the transformation of Taoism into complete theism. He had an ulterior motive in the recovery of his own prestige. In 1005 A.D. the emperor had "lost face" when he was unable to drive the invaders, Ktan Tartars, from his country. He was forced to make a disgraceful peace settlement in which he ceded away large portions of North China. He consulted soothsayers and geomancers for advice. Minister Wang Ch'in-go fabricated a revelation from heaven. The emperor visited the imperial library and consulted the scholars there. In 1008 A.D. he called the ministers together and told them that he had been informed in a dream that heaven was about to send him a letter. The governor of the capitol had just reported seeing a yellow scarf hanging from one of the cornices of the Gate of Heaven. The Emperor went on foot to see the scarf lowered. It contained a letter from a celestial being in the style of Lao-Tzu. In 1012 A.D. it was disclosed that the celestial being was Yu Huang who had not been heard of before the ninth century but now was raised to supremacy.

The people were well-pleased to have many of their favorite folklore gods given imperial recognition. Stories began to circulate. Heaven and hell were added to the system. Paradise was found in various places but mainly in the Three Isles of the Blessed which Chinese folklore had long located in the Eastern Sea. Hell was given every appurtenance of torture and punishment in a place filled with ogres and goblins of every malevolent and horrifying kind. It became the major concern of the living to procure the release of relatives from hell.

There were eight immortals who were believed figures of popular imagination. They were thought to abide either somewhere in the mountains or on the Three Isles of the Blessed. They were supposed to have been human beings who were thought to have been ascetics and had achieved immortality. Though they now lived on in their old bodies, their minds and spirits remained forever young. Four of them were represented as seated together under a pine tree. Two of them sipped wine which was heated by a third. The fourth one played upon a flute for entertainment. The other four were usually portrayed singly.

Tsao Shen is the God of the Hearth and is venerated everywhere in China as the kitchen spirit who sits in the chimney corner watching all that the family says and does. His presence is recalled to naughty children. Food and wine are offered to him on the twenty-fourth day of the twelfth month. Paper money, horses, and chariots are burned together below the chimney and the smoke ascends up the flue to heaven to make an annual report on the behavior of the family.

On New Year, invocations are offered to two Guardians of the Door who are two spirits of great antiquity. They are represented as paper images in military garb, carrying swords or spears. They are attached to the two halves of the front door to ward off the evil spirits during the coming year.

Cheng Huang is the city god who was worshiped in almost every Chinese city but who has lost his official deity.

Taoism has been on the decline for a number of years. The government now frowns on it. Modern education has given it the name of rank superstition. However, the common people cling to it. There was a recrudescence of Taoism during the Boxer Rebellion at the beginning of the twentieth century. Taoism is still rooted deep in the popular mind of the Chinese.

SHINTOISM

CHAPTER 6

SHINTOISM

Shintoism is a prehistoric religion which is found mainly in Japan. Its founder is unknown.

The books most used by the followers of Shintoism, although they are not considered sacred, are: Kojiki (Records of the Ancients), Nihongi (Chronicles of Japan), Yengishiki (Hymns and Prayers).

The followers of Shintoism are often also Buddhists, Taoists, etc.

The Japanese believed two thousand years ago that they were the only people on earth and that their kingdom was the entire earth surrounded by water and small islands. They believed that the sky was near to them and that long ago an arrow was shot from the earth and pierced a hole in the sky and that all the trees, bushes, herbs and all living creatures came through that hole in the sky. The sky they called heaven.

They believed that life in heaven was much like life in Japan – only nicer, and they also believed that there was a world under the earth that wasn't so nice. The entrance to this underworld was once open so that people could visit it, but one day an earthquake closed the entrance with a big stone. Shintoists thought also that there was a bridge to heaven so that people could visit it, but the bridge broke down and was never mended.

The religion of Japan was very simple as there were no images, no sacred books, no commandments and no priests. The people believed that the stars, moon, sun, mountains, rivers, thunder and rain all had spirits that could do either good or evil as they willed. These had to be worshiped to make them do good.

The people also worshiped the Mikado. This was not a human being but was more like the sun, moon, or Mount Fuji that had to be worshiped. The Mikado was a grandson of the Sun-Goddess.

Another story of the creation of Japan was that the Japanese islands were the special creation of various gods which appeared in the heavenly drift-mist and disappeared without event. Finally there came upon the scene two deities who produced the Japanese islands and inhabitants, Izanagi the male and Izanani the female. Their heavenly associates commanded them to "make, consolidate, and give birth to the Japanese islands." They descended the Floating Bridge of Heaven where they reached its lower end. Izanagi pushed down his jeweled spear into the muddy brine and stirred it until the land below them became thick and glutinous – then he drew his spear up. The brine that dripped down from the end of the spear piled up and became an island. Stepping down on the island, they came together and Izanani bore from her womb the eight great islands of Japan. Then they brought into being a populace of thirty-five deities. The last one, Fiery Heart, was the god Kagu-Tsuchi who fatally burned his mother. Izanagi became angry with Kagu-Tsuchi and hacked him up and the other deities were produced out of the flying fragments.

Izanani died and went to the underworld. Izanagi followed, hoping to get her to return to the upper world with him. He was too late as Izanani had begun to decompose and was unsightly. She asked Izanagi not to look at her. He lit the end of the comb which he used to keep his hair in place and saw her lying before him horribly swarming with maggots. She sent the ugly females of Yomi to pursue him and sent eight thunder deities which had been generated from the decay of her own body after him and also sent fifteen hundred warriors of Yomi. She also took up the chase herself.

He fled to the upper world and picked up a rock which it would had taken one thousand men to lift and blocked the pass to the underworld. The two loving deities exchanged angry farewells on opposite sides of the rock.

Izanagi was now covered with pollution. He went down to the ocean to bathe his body. He threw away his staff, girdle, and the rest of his apparel and each item turned into a deity. He stepped into the water as an act of Japanese purification. He washed the filth out of his left eye and produced the most highly revered Japanese deity, Amaterasu, the sun-goddess. The filth from his right eye produced the moon-god, Tsuki-yomi. His nostrils produced the storm god, Susano-wo.

Years later Amaterasu looked down from her seat in heaven and became concerned with the disorder in the islands below. The storm-god's son was ruling. Amaterasu commissioned her grandson, Ni-Ni-Gi to descend to the islands and rule them for her. He obeyed and ruled the islands from the island of Kyushu. Then Ni-Ni-Gi's great grandson, Jimmu-Tenno, the first human emperor, embarked from Kyushu on conquest of the province of Yamamoto where he set up his capitol in 660 B.C.

The whole Japanese people is thought to have descended from the minor deities or lesser Kami residing on the islands.

The emperors of Japan were thought to have descended in an unbroken line from the sun-goddess, Amaterasu.

Japan in its early history was always at war. The soldiers became the heroes of the country. It was an honor to belong to the class of warriors.

The Knights of Japan were patriots and warriors as well as scholars and gentlemen. They used the teachings of Confucius and worked out Rules of Conduct which they called Bushido.

The Ten Ways of a Gentleman are:

1. A gentleman should love justice.
2. A gentleman should have courage.
3. A gentleman should be benevolent.
4. A gentleman is always polite.
5. A gentleman is honorable.
6. A gentleman is loyal.
7. A gentleman has self-control.
8. A gentleman searches for wisdom.
9. A gentleman has love of learning.
10. A gentleman is patriotic.

The Bushido Code of the warrior:

1. Loyalty.

Loyalty was due first of all to the emperor and under him to the lord whom one more immediately serves. One of the most familiar proverbs says, "A loyal retainer does not serve two lords."

2. Gratitude.

Gratitude is a Japanese characteristic but the Christian doctrine that the spring of a right life is not duty but gratitude is one that is readily appreciated by the Japanese.

3. Courage.

The Japanese idea of courage is to be gladly killed in the service of their lord or superiors. In ancient times, a young Japanese warrior wanted to die in battle for his lord and feared nothing so much as dying in bed before he had a chance to sacrifice his life for the object of his devotion.

4. Justice.

The Japanese idea of justice is not allowing any selfishness to stand in the way of one's duty.

5. Truthfulness.

A knight scorns to tell a lie in order to avoid harm or hurt to himself.

6. Politeness.

It is the mark of a strong man to be polite in all circumstances, even to an enemy.

7. Reserve.

Feeling should never be shown no matter how deeply one is moved.

8. Honor.

Death is preferable to disgrace. The knight always carried two swords, a long one to fight his foes and a short one to turn upon his own body in the case of blunder or defeat.

The entire class of followers of Bushido was done away with by the government of Japan in 1868.

Shinto means "way of the Gods." Shintoism is a religio-political system: has neither sacred books nor a moral code; no future state; no paradise or a hell; embraces the Imperial Dynasty of Japan as part of its godhead.

Shintoism is divided into two types of beliefs:

1. State Shinto which before 1945 was subject to national management through a Bureau of Shrines in the Department of Home Affairs. It received a certain degree of support from national, prefectural and local government, supplemented by income from properties, shrine offerings and fees from the sale of charms. Emperor Hirohito renounced his divinity in 1946 after Japan's defeat in World War II. The purpose of State Shinto was to teach patriotism and it became an official government cult.

2. Sectarian Shinto was managed by the Bureau of Religions in the Department of Education. It depended entirely for its support upon the voluntary contributions of its adherents and income from properties.

There were three main cultural stages in the evolution of Shintoism: the stage of primitive nature worship; the stage of higher nature worship or sheer polytheism, and the advanced cultural religion wherein beliefs and practices relating to Kami objects have come under the influence of ethical and intellectual influences of a high order.

Ancestor worship has had a place in Shintoism from the early times to the present.

Japanese authorities do not know the meaning of Kami. Some Japanese believe that it means "superior being," especially superior men. Shinto became primarily an ancestor worship cult culminating in adoration of a living god. Others believe that Kami is a "mysterious being." Shinto becomes fundamentally a belief in spirits and their worship. Others believe that the term sets forth the ancient and persistent tendency toward panpsychism on the part of the Japanese people, which made Shinto essentially pantheism.

The Imperial Rescript on Education in 1890, when anti-western sentiment was running high, made a flawless epitome of a peerless Japanese nationalism:

"Know ye, Our Subjects:

"Our Imperial ancestors have founded our empire on a basis broad and everlasting, and have deeply and firmly implanted virtue: Our Subjects, ever united in loyalty and filial piety, have, from generation to generation, illustrated the beauty thereof. This is the glory of the fundamental character of our empire, and herein lies also the source of our education. Ye, our subjects, be filial to your parents, affectionate to your brothers and sisters; as husband and wives be harmonious, as friends true; bear yourselves in modesty and moderation; extend your benevolence to all; pursue learning and cultivate arts, and thereby develop intellectual faculties and perfect moral powers; furthermore, advance the public good and promote common interests; always respect the constitution and observe the laws; should emergency arise, offer yourselves courageously to the State; and thus guard and maintain the prosperity of Our Imperial Throne coeval with heaven and earth. So shall ye not only be our good and faithful subjects but follow the best traditions of your forefathers.

"The way here set forth is indeed the teaching bequeathed by Our Imperial Ancestors to be observed alike by their descendants and the subjects, infallible in all ages and true in all places. It is our wish to lay it to heart in all reverence, in common with you, our subjects."

Shintoism glorifies war and makes every appeal to arms that has been sanctified by the will of the emperor a holy crusade. It fosters convictions of racial and national superiority and frustrates genuine international cooperation by making Japanese national sovereignty absolute and complete. It makes the chief end of education the inculcation of unquestioning obedience and destroys any prospect of building a cooperative human society.

The written constitution of 1889 declared that the emperor was "sacred and inviolable," but this doctrine was abolished in 1945 with the defeat of Japan in World War II. Shintoism is still retained by some of the older people as it has been so ingrained with Japanese nationalism for centuries.

There were 110,000 Shinto shrines set aside and nationalized by the government before 1945. There were also many unlisted wayside shrines which were too small to be mentioned in the records of the Department of Home Affairs and were too remote to be readily accessible. Many were memorial in character and were dedicated to legendary heroes or ancient clan figures. Others were small temples erected in honor of messengers and symbols of the grain goddess, Inari. Others were placed in factory compounds and on the roofs of department stores. These shrines were served by 16,000 priests who were appointed by the government and were officially instructed not to conduct religious ceremonies such as funerals. The most honored state shrine before 1945 was the Grand Imperial Shrine at Ise which was dedicated to the sun-goddess, Amaterasu. The Japanese made a pilgrimage to the shrine "once in a lifetime."

The O'Harai was the Great Purification which was performed at Ise and a number of other shrines twice a year in June and December. This was a national purgation by a purification ritual when the priests sought to attain an inward as well as an outward cleanliness by abstaining from all food. The priests waved an urica or purification wand above the people and read the ritual and accepted the penalty offerings. The people rubbed their bodies against straw or paper effigies representing themselves, which were supposed to transfer their guilt to their substitutes. Then the priests collected and threw the effigies into some body of water – lake, river or ocean – and the guilt of the people was thus borne away. The emperor or descendant of the forgiving sun-goddess pronounced from the imperial capitol the absolution of sins and the impurities of the nation.

ZOROASTRIANISM

CHAPTER 7

ZOROASTRIANISM

Zoroastrianism was founded in the sixth century B.C. in ancient Persia (now Iran) by Zoroaster, whose Greek name was Zarathustra. There are two possible dates ascribed to the life of Zoroaster – 660-583 B.C. and 570-500 B.C. We have accepted the first date which seems more historically accurate.

The sacred books of Zoroastrianism are the Avestas, which contain hymns, a section of liturgy and the codes of purity.

Zoroastrianism is a small sect numbering only about 125,000 in the world, with most settled now in the Bombay area of India and called Parsees (Persians). There are few which have remained in Persia.

Zoroaster was the son of Porushasp of the Spitama clan and his beautiful wife, Daighdova. His birthplace has been in controversy but the most popular theory is that he was born in Azerbaigan, west of the Caspian Sea.

There are many stories concerning the birth of Zoroaster. One of these stories is worth repeating. Durasan, the chief magician of Iran, began to tremble in great fear as he had a vision that a child was born who would grow up to destroy the magic and idol worship and would banish all the magicians from the land. Durasan sent three magicians to bring the child Zoroaster to him in the Fire Temple where he had prepared a great fire on the altar. He placed the child in the center of the fire and left the temple.

Zoroaster's mother came home and found the baby gone. She ran to the Fire Temple to pray and there she found her son playing happily in the midst of the flames as if he was splashing about in a luke warm bath.

Durasan was certain that Zoroaster was no ordinary child. He called his three magicians and ordered them to get Zoroaster and place him in the middle of the highway where a large herd of cattle was to pass. The first cow ran up to the child, stepped over him in a manner to protect him. The entire herd passed over him without harming him. For three days and nights Durasan planned and plotted means of getting rid of Zoroaster. He was placed in a wolves' den. The wolves did not harm Zoroaster and goats disguised as angels appeared to feed the baby.

When Zoroaster was seven years old, he was sent to study under Burzin-Kusus, whose wisdom was known throughout Iran. He studied for eight years under Burzin-Kusus. He not only studied religion but farming, cattle-raising, and healing. Zoroaster returned home and put on the Sacred Shirt and Sacred Girdle which was the symbol of being confirmed into the religion of his people.

Iran was invaded by the Turanians of the neighboring country soon after Zoroaster's return home. He volunteered, went out into the battle fields and applied his knowledge of healing to the wounded soldiers.

Famine broke out in Iran after the war. Sickness and the need in the land was as great as in war and Zoroaster worked among the sick and poor. He worked among these people for five years and his father wanted him to get married, settle down and become a land-owner and cattle raiser. Zoroaster married a beautiful girl, Havovee, but he would not settle down. His experience in the war and famine convinced him that he was destined for a greater work.

Zoroaster worked for ten more years among the poor and needy, constantly planning methods to alleviate the sufferings of his people. The sorrow and misfortune of his people seemed to have no end. He wondered where all the evil in the world came from and reasoned that if he could find the cause of evil, he could cure it.

Zoroaster decided to become a hermit to think of good and evil in the hope of discovering the source of suffering in the world. He went to Mount Sabalan, determined not to return home until he had gained the wisdom he was seeking.

Zoroaster remained alone as he thought of the teachings of Burzin-Kursus, of his father and the priests. He thought of his experience in war and famine but he could not find one explanation of evil. He was about ready to return home to his wife when he watched the sunset and the realization came to him that the day was divided into day and night – light and darkness. This fact was known to him all his life but now it seemed to be the Key of Wisdom.

He thought of the comparison of good and evil – light and darkness. Day and night can never change their nature, so good can never become evil or evil can never become good. Good must always be good and evil must always be evil. The magicians and idol-worshiping priests were wrong to pray to the good gods to do evil to their enemies and for the evil gods to do good.

Then Zoroaster thought that the world must be ruled by two forces – good and evil. He named the good force, Ahura Mazada, and the evil force he called Angra Manyu.

Zoroaster was still in doubt as to why good and evil were created or how people ought to live to overcome evil and suffering.

He remained on Mount Sabalan to clarify his thoughts and to work out a solution for overcoming the problem of evil and suffering. When he came down from the mount, he was ready to proclaim the truth about good and evil to his people. The people of Iran were not ready to listen to him. They were used to worshiping gods and idols that could be seen. Zoroaster's conception of good and evil could not be seen, heard or touched.

Zoroaster's family rejected his teaching. In the next ten years, Zoroaster gained but one convert – his cousin. His teaching was too hard for the common people to understand so he sought audience with the educated class who would be able to think it through.

He went to see King Vishtaspa and was refused entrance to the royal palace by the Guardian of the Gates. Zoroaster commanded entrance with a voice of authority and the Guardian of the Gates who was frightened went to see the king and Zoroaster was shown in.

Zoroaster addressed the king in a firm voice:

"I, Zoroaster Spitama, prophet of the one wise Lord, have come to you, mighty king, to turn your heart from vain and evil idols toward the glory of the true wise and eternal Lord!

"I teach the word of Truth against the word of Falsehood. If you or your wise men wish to question me, I shall answer and prove your ways of idol-worship to be wrong and shadowed with the darkness of night, and the way of the one wise Lord, Ahura Mazda, to be good and bright as the light of day.

"If you find my words to be true, promise that you will abandon the dark ways of idol-worship and follow the shining word of the wise Lord."

The king promised and his wise men engaged Zoroaster in a three days' debate. The king accepted Zoroaster's teachings and made him the high priest in the Royal Palace. Many Iranians accepted Zoroaster's teachings due to the testimony of the king.

The court magicians and idol-worshiping priests plotted against Zoroaster. They planted many items in Zoroaster's room to show that he was a sorcerer. The king had Zoroaster arrested and put into prison.

The king's favorite horse became sick. All the magicians, priests and physicians could not heal it. Zoroaster sent word from the prison that he could heal the horse. Zoroaster exacted a promise from the king that if he healed the horse the king would accept his teachings and never depart from them. Zoroaster rubbed one withered leg of the horse and it was restored.

The king ordered 12,000 cows to be killed and the hides tanned, bound with gold rings and ordered the scribes to write down the teachings of Zoroaster. This became the Avesta – the sacred book of Zoroastrianism.

Zoroaster's daughter, Porucista, was proclaimed the wisest woman of the kingdom. She married the Prime Minister of Balkh and Zoroaster's position was secured with the prime minister as a son-in-law. Zoroaster began to spread his teachings to the whole world. He became known all over Iran and his teachings passed into Turan, Greece, and India.

The Iranians were in debt to the kingdom of Turan. Zoroaster asked the king to send a message to Turan that if they refused to give up their idol-worshiping and accept the teachings of Zoroastrianism, that the debt would not be paid.

Turan replied that if the Iranians refused to give up the teachings of Zoroaster and return to the teachings of their forefathers that they would be attacked.

War followed and the Iranians under Zoroaster were victorious Zoroaster became a hero and his teachings were acccepted.

Turan hated Zoroaster and planned revenge. They plotted against Zoroaster and the Iranians for seventeen years. They attacked Iran and beseiged the city of Balkh and captured it. Zoroaster was killed by the Turanian soldiers who stabbed him in the back as he prayed in the temple for the victory of his people.

King Vishtaspa vowed to avenge the death of Zoroaster. He defeated Turan and refused them peace until they accepted Zoroastrianism. He then sent missionaries to other fields.

The three preeminent features of Zoroastrianism are:

1. Zoroaster rejected the numerous gods worshiped by his fellow countrymen and elevated one, Ahura Mazda, later known as Ormuzd, to the place of a supreme god.

2. Zoroaster declared that God was good. The Spirit of Evil Angra Manyu, later called Ahriman, was the very antithesis of Ahura Mazda and the two were in constant struggle.

3. There is to be a great day of judgment when every individual must stand on his own record in that day. The good is to be rewarded and the evil is to suffer in torment.

The principal feature of modern Zoroastrianism is the fire cult

This worship is conducted secretly and no outsider is ever permitted to witness it. It is performed in the midst of the Fire Temple by properly ordained and ritually prepared representatives of the priesthood. The ceremonial requisite of kindling of the temple fire is elaborate. It is made by compounding sixteen different fires – each purified by an exceedingly involved ritual. The fires must be secured by kindling one from the other successively 91 times to the accompaniment of prayers. The priest must cover his face lest his breath pollute the sacred flame.

The ritual prayers are recited in the Avestan language of the sacred book and 90% of the Zoroastrians do not understand it.

Men and women have equal privileges in the place of worship.

Anyone touching a corpse must immediately be purified by ablutions with water or with the urine of cattle. Corpses have always been so defiling that they are not allowed to enter the earth lest they corrupt the ground, nor fall into the water lest they render it unfit for any use, nor be burned on a funeral pyre lest they defile the flame. They are placed in stone "Towers of Silence" open to the sky so that birds of prey may feast on them. Any portion of a dead body, or for that matter, any part severed from a living body, as for example nail-parings or hair cut from the head or beard, is unclean. Spitting, especially in the presence of another person, is forbidden. Exhaled breath is defiling – priests wear cloths over their faces while tending the sacred fires. Creatures which feed on dead flesh, such as maggots, flies and ants are loathed. Direct contact with any of them require that the person involved must be cleansed and purified without delay.

Much attention is paid in Zoroastrianism to its doctrine of the future life. Zoroastrianists teach that individual judgment takes place the fourth day after death. The first three nights the soul of the dead person sits at the head of its former body and meditates on the past good or evil thoughts, words and deeds. He is comforted by the good angels if righteous and tormented by demons if he has been wicked. On the fourth day, the soul goes to the Chinvat bridge to stand before its judges (Mithra and his associates, Sraosha and Rashnu), judgment is rendered and the sentence is passed. The soul then walks out onto the Chinvat Bridge. It walks to the middle of the bridge where sharp edges stand like a sword. Hell is below. The soul is carried to the sharp edge. If righteous, the sharp edge presents the broad side. If wicked, it continues edgewise. The soul takes three steps forward, for the evil thoughts, evil words, and evil deeds which it has performed. It is cut down from the head of the bridge and falls headlong into hell. The righteous soul is guided over the bridge by its own conscience in the form of a beautiful maiden.

If the merits or demerits balance exactly, the soul is sent to Hamestakan which is located between the earth and the stars.

Hell, according to Zoroastrianism, has several elevations. The lowest depth is in the bowels of the earth where darkness can be grasped by the hand and where the stench is unbearable. Heaven also has ascending levels corresponding to good thoughts, good words, and good deeds which are located respectively in the regions of the stars, moon and sun. The good soul passes on until it reaches the highest heaven called Garotman or Garo-demana.

At the appearance of Soshyana, all the dead will be raised. Heaven and hell will be emptied of their residents, which will make up the great assembly where final judgment will be passed upon all souls. The righteous and wicked will be separated. A flood of molten metal will pour out upon the earth and roar through hell, purifying all the regions with its scorching fires. Every living soul will have to walk through the flaming river. To the righteous it will seem like warm milk as there is no evil in them to be burned. It will bring terrible agony to the wicked as all the evil will be burned out of them. There will be a final conflict when Ahura Mazda and his angels will hurl Ahriman and his devils into the flames and they will be utterly consumed. All the survivors of the fiery trial will live together in the new heavens and the new earth in utmost joy and felicity. The adults will remain forever at forty years of age and the children at fifteen. Friends and relatives will be reunited forever.

The six attributes of Ahura Mazda are: Good Mind, Good Order, Wisdom, Piety, Well-being and Immortality.

Zoroaster taught that the world would come to an end in his own day. He taught that the wise Lord created the world in six periods of two months each. The world would last for a thousand years for each month of creation. Zoroaster was supposedly born at the end of 9,000 years from creation. Three thousand years after Zoroaster's death a son of his would appear on earth. This son would be the Sayoshani – the Messiah – the saviour of mankind.

Zoroaster was the first religious leader to teach belief in an abstract god – a god one could not touch, see or hear.

Zoroaster urged his followers to fight the battle of the Wise Lord through: purity of thought, word and deed; cleanliness; charity of heart; kindliness to useful animals; doing profitable work; and helping people who cannot afford it to get a good education.

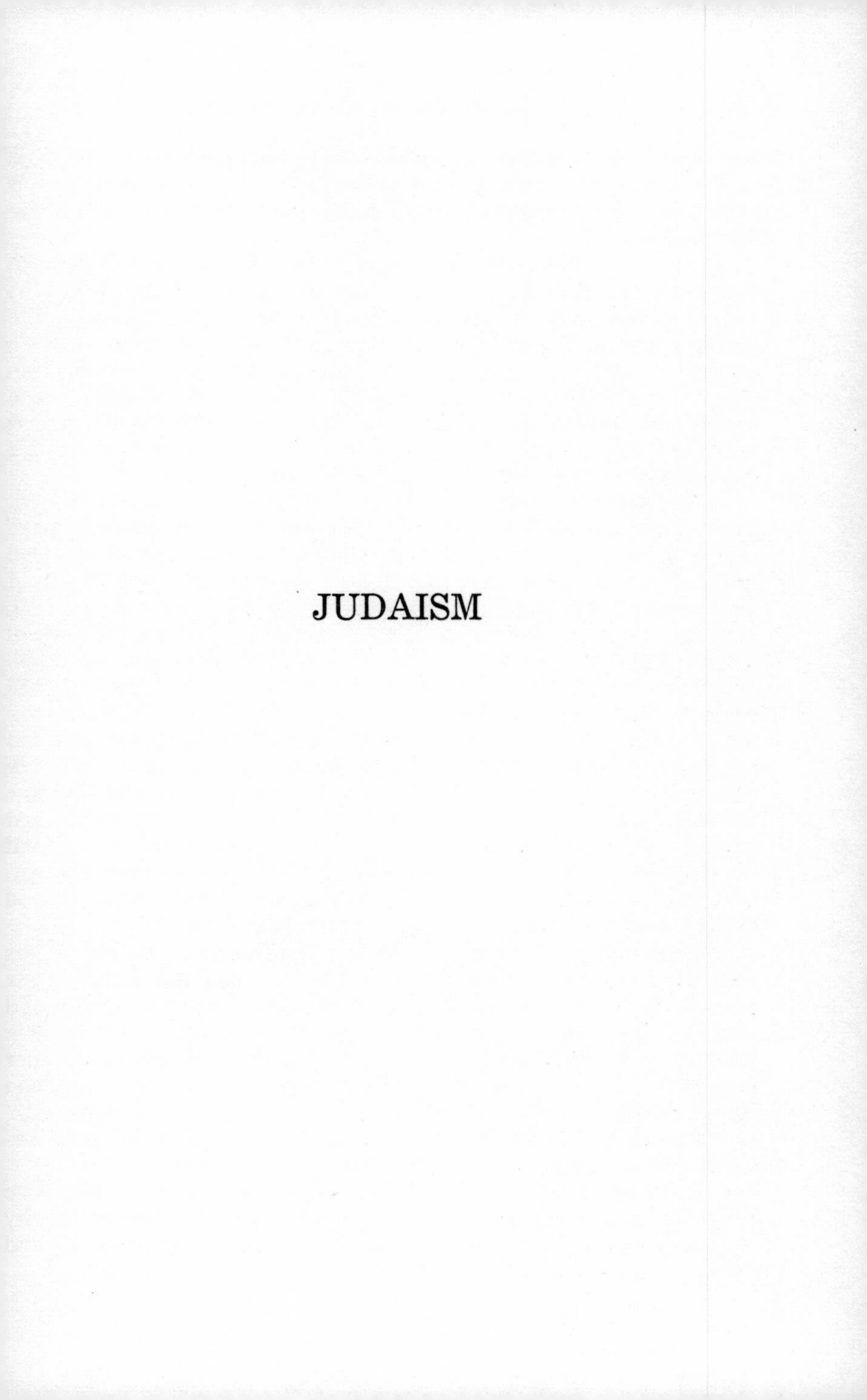

JUDAISM

CHAPTER 8

JUDAISM

Judaism was founded in the thirteenth century B.C. by a succession of prophets such as Moses, Abraham, Isaiah, Jeremiah, Amos, Hosea, etc. Moses and Abraham have been given the principle credit for establishing the system.

The sacred books of Judaism are the Old Testament, of which the first five books of Moses are considered the most sacred, and The Talmud and its commentaries.

The history of Judaism is a history of the Jewish race.

There was in the city of Ur a man named Terah who was an idol worshiper and idol-maker. He made idols of all shapes and sizes which he sold to the people of the land.

Terah had three sons, Abraham, Nahor, and Haran, who were shepherds in the green pasturelands of the Euphrates valley.

One day Abraham was left alone in his father's shop. He took an ax and smashed all the idols but one. He placed the ax in the hand of the one remaining idol. He told his father that the idol with the ax had smashed the other idols.

It was no longer safe for Abraham to remain home and question the idol worship of his father. He took his wife, some of his relatives, servants, sheep, and cattle and wandered north toward the land called Canaan.

Abraham had two sons, Isaac and Ishmael. Isaac was the son of Abraham's wife, Sarah; and Ishmael was the son of an Egyptian handmaid, Hagar. Ishmael was the forerunner of the Arabs. Isaac had a son, Jacob, whose name was later changed to Israel and his children were called Israelites. Jacob had twelve sons who all had large families and the Israelites became a large and powerful tribe.

There came a great famine in Canaan and the Israelites decided to go down to Egypt where they had heard there was plenty of food and pasture. They settled in Goshen close to the Nile River.

The Israelites were made the slaves of the Egyptians, but still they refused to worship the idols. A law was passed that all the

Israelite boys should be drowned. It was thought that this would destroy the race as the Israelite girls would be forced to marry Egyptian husbands.

An Israelite boy by the name of Moses was born. He was hidden in his mother's house for three months and then placed in a basket in the river, where he was found by the king's daughter who hired the boy's own mother to raise him in the palace. Thus he received a good education.

Moses finally found out that he was an Israelite and began to think of how he could free his people from the bondage of the Egyptians. He killed an Egyptian who was beating two Israelite slaves.

Moses ran away to Midian to hide. There he married Zipporah, daughter of Jethro, and helped his father-in-law in tending his sheep. He continually thought of the cruel hardships of his people in Egypt. One day he left his wife and children in Midian and returned to Egypt with the hope of freeing his people. He appeared with his brother, Aaron, before the king of Egypt, to seek the release of the Israelites.

The king refused to grant freedom to Moses' people. Plagues then came upon Egypt which changed the king's mind and he finally released the Israelites.

Moses led his people out of Egypt and went up into Mt. Sinai where God gave him the Ten Commandments. God miraculously provided food and water for the Israelites on their long journey out of Egypt. They gained courage as they believed that Jehovah their God was fighting their battles and watching over them.

The Hebrews were first ruled for 300 years by judges who were military leaders. The twelve tribes of Israel were organized into a kingdom with Saul as its first king. There were only three kings, Saul, David and Solomon, of the United Kingdom. The glory of Israel reached its height during Solomon's reign.

Solomon built a temple in Jerusalem where he placed the Holy of Holies in which Jehovah their God was supposed to dwell.

Saul established the kingdom; David strengthened it; and Solomon enriched it.

Then the Kingdom was divided. The Kingdom of Israel occupied the northern portion of the land while the Kingdom of Judah occupied the southern half. This greatly weakened the Jews against their enemies. The Assyrians conquered the Kingdom of Israel in the north. The people were taken captive to other lands. They have never been heard of again and they are referred to as the Ten Lost Tribes of Israel.

The Kingdom of Judah was captured by the Babylonians 160 years later. The Babylonians burned the temple in Jerusalem and carried the people captive into Babylon.

In their own land the Hebrews had thought of Jehovah as the God of Palestine, but now they thought of Him as being with their people not only in Palestine but also in captivity.

Persia conquered Babylon about fifty years after Babylon had conquered Judah. The Persians called the people of Judah, Jehudis, from which the word Jews and the religion of Judaism is derived.

The Persians were friendly toward the Jews. King Cyrus permitted them to return to their land and rebuild their kingdom. The Jews studied the Persian religion and learned many things from it. They learned from Zoroastrianism that the Persians believed that the world was ruled by two forces: the good and wise Lord and the evil spirit. The Jews could not conceive of the creator divided in two as they believed that only one God created both light and darkness, joy and sorrow, good and evil.

Now the Jews concluded that Jehovah must be one God who created the universe. The Jews learned of heaven and hell from Zoroastrianism. They changed their outlook concerning the coming of the Messiah.

Zoroastrianism taught that the Messiah would not be a national hero to bring glory and power to Persia but a Messiah who would redeem all mankind from the power of the evil spirit. The Jews were looking for a Messiah who would be a national hero, a descendant of King David, who would restore the United Hebrew Kingdom as it was in the day of David and Solomon.

The Jews now began to think of their Messiah as more than a national hero who would bring peace and happiness to all mankind. Having returned to Palestine with the help of King Cyrus, they rebuilt their holy temple in Jerusalem. But their religion had changed.

Ezra, the scribe, began collecting the history, legends, and laws of the Jews into a book, The Talmud, which became the sacred scriptures of Judaism.

The Jews suffered oppression again. A weak, small, defenseless nation, they were easily conquered by the Greeks and then by the Romans who ruled them with an iron hand.

The Jews became more hopeful that their Redeemer or Messiah

would come as the oppression grew more intense. Jesus, the Messiah, came in this period, but was rejected by the Jews since He did not set up an earthly kingdom as the Jews thought the Messiah would. Jesus came with a lowly birth while the Jews were looking for the Messiah to come as a conquering hero to set them free from their captors.

Jerusalem was again destroyed in 70 A.D. and the Jews were scattered over many lands.

Present-day Jews are classified in several groups:

Orthodox Jews are the most zealous to preserve the traditions of Judaism. The real basis for the religious faith and practice of the Orthodox Jews is the Talmud and its commentaries. These Jews have a degree of reverence for the Old Testament but divine inspiration is only ascribed to the writings of Moses. The hope of a coming nationalistic Messiah still persists although it is blurred.

The Reformed Jews attempt to adapt Judaism to the demands of modern life. They have abandoned much of Jewish tradition, preach an ethical monotheism, and conduct their worship in the language of the nation in which they are living. Little attention is paid to Sabbath observance. Reformed Judaism is composed largely of wealthy Jews. There is less interest in God's Word and they are more open to new ideas.

The Conservative Jews follow a middle position between the Orthodox and Reformed Jews. They have held to many of the ancient traditions of Judaism, but have discarded what they consider nonessential.

The Zionist Jews are most interested in returning to Palestine. Not all Jews are Zionists, as many of them are satisfied in the countries of their dispersion. Zionism is the strongest passion among the Jews of today.

The Jews reject the doctrine of the trinity and they use Deuteronomy 6:4, "Hear, O Israel, the Lord our God is one Lord," as the cornerstone of their doctrine.

Rabbi Moses ben Maimon (1135-1204), also known as Maimonides, formulated the Thirteen Principles of Faith which are the chief tenets of Orthodox Judaism:

1. I believe with perfect faith that the Creator, blessed be His name, is the author and guide of everything that has been created, and that He alone has made, does make, and will make all things.

2. I believe with perfect faith that the Creator, blessed be His name, is a unity, and that there is no unity in any manner like unto His, and that He alone is our God, who was, is and will be.

3. I believe with perfect faith that the Creator, blessed be His name, is not a body and that He is free from all the accidents of matter, and that He has not any form whatsoever.

4. I believe with perfect faith that the Creator, blessed be His name, is the first and the last.

5. I believe with perfect faith that the Creator, blessed be His name, is He to whom alone it is right to pray, and that it is not right to pray to any beside Him.

6. I believe with perfect faith that all the words of the prophets are true.

7. I believe with perfect faith that the prophecy of Moses, our teacher, peace be unto him, was true, and that he was the chief of the prophets, both of those that preached and of those that follow him.

8. I believe with perfect faith that the whole law now in our possession, is the same that was given to Moses, our teacher, peace be unto him.

9. I believe with perfect faith that this law will not be changed, and that there will never be any other law from the Creator, blessed be His name.

10. I believe with perfect faith that the Creator, blessed be His name, knows every deed of the children of men, and all their thoughts as it is said. It is He that fashioneth the hearts of them all, that giveth heed to all their deeds.

11. I believe with perfect faith that the Creator, blessed be His name, rewards those that keep His commandments, and punishes those that transgress them.

12. I believe with perfect faith that there will be a resurrection of the dead at the time when it shall please the Creator, blessed be His name, and exalted be the remembrance of Him forever and ever.

13. I believe with perfect faith in the coming of the Messiah, and though He tarry, I will wait daily for His coming.

The Jews had been given a picture of the coming Messiah many years before He came. They failed to recognize the Messiah that was predicted by the prophets. The Old Testament gives a complete picture of Jesus which was completely fulfilled in the New Testament, but the Jews rejected this.

Several of these prophecies should be studied:

1. The Messiah was to be born in Bethlehem. Micah 5:2
2. The Messiah was to be born of a virgin. Isaiah 7:14

3. The Messiah was to be a prophet like Moses. Deuteronomy 18:15, 18, 19
4. The Messiah was to enter Jerusalem in triumph. Zechariah 9:9
5. The Messiah was to be rejected by His own people. Isaiah 53:1, 3; Psalm 118:22
6. The Messiah was to be betrayed by one of His followers. Psalm 41:9
7. The Messiah was to be tried and condemned. Isaiah 53:8
8. The Messiah was to be silent before His accusers. Isaiah 53:7
9. The Messiah was to be smitten and spit upon by His enemies. Micah 5:1; Isaiah 50:6
10. The Messiah was to be mocked and taunted. Psalm 22:7, 8
11. The Messiah was to die by crucifixion. Psalm 22:14, 16, 17
12. The Messiah was to suffer with transgressors and pray for His enemies. Isaiah 53:12
13. The Messiah was to be given vinegar and gall. Psalm 69:21
14. The Messiah's garments were to be divided by casting lots. Psalm 22:18
15. The Messiah's bones were not to be broken. Numbers 9:12; Exodus 12:46
16. The Messiah was to die as a sacrifice for sin. Isaiah 53:5, 6, 8, 10, 11, 12
17. The Messiah was to be raised from the dead. Psalm 16:10
18. The Messiah was to take His place at God's right hand. Psalm 110:1

The prophecies which were given to the Jews in the Old Testament were completely fulfilled in Jesus Christ. Though the Messiah has come, the Jews are still looking for His first coming.

No nation nor religion has suffered the severe persecutions that have been the lot of the Jewish people, yet they have never lost their identity. They have been scattered throughout the world, yet they have remained Jewish. They have not been assimilated into the countries of the world. There is a strong Zionist movement under way at the present time and thousands of Jews are returning to their homeland, Israel, since it became a nation again in 1948.

CHRISTIANITY

CHAPTER 9

CHRISTIANITY

Christianity was founded by Jesus Christ. The birthday of the Christian Church was the Day of Pentecost in 33 A.D., although the message of the coming of the Messiah was written many years before in the Old Testament. The New Testament was a fulfillment of the Old Testament.

The Sacred Scriptures of Christianity is the Bible – both the Old and New Testaments. The Old Testament, except for a difference in order, is the same as the Hebrew Scriptures. The New Testament contains the story of the life and ministry of Christ in the four gospels, the establishment of the church in the book of Acts, the letters of instruction to the Christians in the epistles, and the prophecy of things yet to come in the book of Revelation.

The Jews believed that from the time Moses led the Jews out of Egypt, Jehovah would send a Redeemer or Messiah. They were given a clear picture of what to look for in the Messiah when He came but they rejected Jesus when God sent Him as the long awaited Messiah.

There was a period of 400 years between the Old and the New Testaments when God did not raise up a prophet to proclaim the coming of the Messiah.

The Jews were being bitterly persecuted under the reign of Augustus Caesar and their hope for the coming of the Messiah increased. They were looking for a national hero who would free them from their oppression and bondage. The true ruler of Judea was Augustus Caesar, the Roman Emperor. King Herod was the ruler of Judea appointed by Caesar and he wanted to retain his position forever. Any talk of a coming Messiah angered him as he thought that one would come who would dethrone him.

Herod was seventy years old when Christ was born. He sent spies to find Christ that He might be killed to prevent Him from assuming the earthly throne of Judea. The spies found Christ in Bethlehem after searching for Him in Jerusalem, but they did not return to tell Herod where Christ was born. This angered Herod. The prophet had prophesied that Christ would be born in Bethlehem (Micah 5:2).

In hope of killing Christ, Herod issued an edict that all the Hebrew boys under two years of age were to be killed. An angel appeared to Joseph, the foster father of Christ, and ordered him to flee to Egypt with Christ and His mother, Mary, to avoid the wrath of Herod.

An angel appeared again to Joseph in Egypt after the death of Herod. Joseph, Mary and Christ returned to Nazareth, a small town in lower Galilee, far from the highways of the world, fifty-five miles from Jerusalem. Joseph taught Christ all the Holy Commandments as he was too poor to send Jesus to the schools in Jerusalem.

When Jesus was twelve years of age, He was taken to Jerusalem where He astonished the learned men with His wisdom.

Jesus began His public ministry when He was thirty years of age. John the Baptist had been preaching the message, "Repent for the kingdom of God is at hand." After Jesus appeared to John and was baptized in the Jordan River, He started His preaching ministry.

Jesus chose twelve men whom He personally trained to carry on His message. These men were of humble birth, completely dedicated to their Lord and to the message which they were presenting to the people.

The first converts to Christianity were won by personal contact. Andrew was a follower of John the Baptist and when Jesus came with His public ministry, Andrew followed Him. Then Andrew went out and found his brother, Peter, whom he led to the Saviour. Philip came to Christ and then went out to lead Nathaniel to the Messiah (John 1:39-51).

John the Baptist, the forerunner of Christ, was beheaded for preaching against the sins of King Herod Antipas, the son of Herod the Great. The followers of Jesus suffered severe persecutions and ridicule and many of them met their deaths as martyrs.

The Pharisees were the enemies of Christ. They wanted the people to go back to the religion of the Jews before their exile to Babylon. They did not believe in heaven and hell nor did they believe in life after death. They opposed any teaching which was contrary to the Mosaic law or the teachings of the early prophets.

Jesus denounced the Pharisees openly and warned the people against them and the gap between Jesus and the religious leaders widened.

Judaism taught the observance of the Mosaic law, while Jesus came teaching the law of love. This was difficult for the Jews to accept after all the bitter persecutions which they had endured.

Jesus was betrayed by one of His disciples, Judas Iscariot, and was handed over to the Roman soldiers, tried, crucified, and buried. But He rose again from the grave as He had told His followers that He would.

Christianity is the only religion in the world which claims that its founder arose from the grave and is now living.

The Resurrection of Christ gave His followers the courage which they needed to carry on the message of Christ. When Jesus was arrested and tried, His followers deserted Him and hid for fear of their own lives. Now that He had arisen, they came boldly out of hiding and were ready to carry His message throughout the world.

The enemies of Christ were not concerned with killing Jesus personally, but they were concerned with stamping out the teachings which He was propagating.

After the Resurrection and Ascension of Christ, Saul of Tarsus, who was one of the most feared persecutors of the followers of Christ, was remarkably converted outside the city of Damascus (Acts 9). He was on his way from Jerusalem to Damascus to persecute the Christians, but when he reached Damascus he now believed the message which he had come to destroy.

Saul's name was changed to Paul and he became the outstanding missionary and preacher of the message which Christ had presented. Paul was a learned man who had been educated in the best Jewish schools of his day. After his conversion, he went to Arabia where he stayed for three years, apparently in communion with God. He returned to Jerusalem, but was rejected by the other apostles who knew of his early efforts at persecution. Finally he was accepted and began a ministry which established companies of believers throughout the then known world. He wrote letters of instruction to these new companies of believers. These are the epistles of the New Testament and the guide to all Christians. His letters deal with specific problems which arose in the Early Church and which are prevalent in the present-day churches.

Jerusalem was the first church which was established and became the headquarters of the early believers. Then a church was established in Antioch. There the believers were first called Christians which was given as a title of derision to the followers of Christ.

Nearly all the early converts to Christianity were Jewish. Nearly all the writers of the New Testament were Jewish-Christians. A problem arose as to whether a convert would have to become a Jew by being circumcised and keeping the Mosaic law in order to become a Christian. A council was called at Jerusalem (Acts 15) to settle this problem. Christianity was not a sect within Judaism but was entirely separate from Judaism.

Paul was confronted with the same problem among the churches of Galatia. He had preached throughout Galatia and many of the heathen there had accepted Christ as their personal Saviour. After Paul left, a group of Judaizers came to Galatia to tell the people that Paul had presented an incomplete message and they would have to be circumcised and keep the Mosaic law in order to be saved. He wrote the epistle to the Galatians to explain the Christian doctrine of justification by faith apart from keeping the Mosaic law. He used the teaching of the Old Testament to present the doctrines of Christianity.

Jesus came to present a personal message instead of one that was bound by tradition. He presented the essence of Christianity in John 3 when He personally dealt with a pious Jew, Nicodemus, regarding his personal salvation. Nicodemus was an educated, respected Jew. He had seen or heard of the miracles which Jesus had performed and was convinced that He was the Messiah, because God must had been with Him to enable Him to perform these miracles. Jesus presented the doctrine of the "new birth." Every man or woman had inherited the sin of Adam and the only solution to the sin problem and personal salvation was the acceptance of Christ by faith.

The message of Christianity is so simple that it is difficult for many people to accept it. There is a tendency for the average person to want to do something to obtain salvation. Christianity is entirely by faith and not by works (Ephesians 2:8, 9).

The chief doctrines of Christianity are summed up in the Apostles' Creed:

"I believe in God, the Father almighty, creator of heaven and earth: and in Jesus Christ, His only Son, our Lord; who was conceived by the Holy Ghost, born of the virgin Mary, suffered under Pontius Pilate, was crucified, died, and was buried. He descended into hell; the third day He arose again from the dead; He ascended into heaven, sitteth at the right hand of God, the Father almighty; from thence He shall come to judge the living and the dead. I believe in the Holy Ghost, the universal Christian Church, the communion of saints, the forgiveness of sins, the resurrection of the body, and life everlasting. Amen."

The Bible is the rule of faith and practice for the Christian. Paul wrote, "All scripture is given by inspiration of God, and is profitable for doctrine, for reproof, for correction, for instruction in righteousness: that the man of God may be perfect, throughly furnished unto all good works" (II Timothy 3:16, 17).

Christianity is a personal religion. A sinner to become a Christian must accept the person of Jesus Christ as his own personal Saviour. No one can become a Christian by merely conforming to a certain creed or by joining a certain group or church.

All mankind has inherited a sinful nature. "For all have sinned, and come short of the glory of God; being justified freely by his grace through the redemption that is in Christ Jesus" (Romans 3: 23, 34).

Salvation can only come through the personal acceptance of Jesus Christ as the sinner's personal Saviour. "For the wages of sin is death; but the gift of God is eternal life through Jesus Christ our Lord" (Romans 6:23).

Christianity has been carried throughout the world by Christian missionaries. It has met with bitter persecution and opposition through the years, but the message has transformed the lives of men and women through the ages. Head-hunters have become civilized members of society. Drunkards have been sobered and have become respected husbands and fathers. There has not been a problem which the Gospel of Christ was not able to right.

Christianity under the Roman Empire was persecuted chiefly on three grounds: (1) The Romans thought that the Christians were unpatriotic because they foretold the fall of the Empire, would not sacrifice to the emperor and refused to perform military service or accept state offices; (2) the Christians were considered anti-social because they did not participate in the Roman festivals; and (3) they were considered immoral because families sometimes broke up when one became Christianized.

There were several heresies which crept into the early church. These led it away from the teachings of Christ and the Apostles:

1. Arianism was a purely monotheistic belief which denied the divinity of Christ and claimed that He was only human.

2. Gnosticism denied the humanity of Christ and proclaimed Him as a phantom spirit who came from the Supreme Being to give enlightenment and knowledge to mankind.

3. Catharism in the eleventh and twelfth centuries believed in

the dualism of God – a god of good and a god of evil. The God of Evil was identified with Jehovah of the Old Testament and was connected with pestilence, war and matter. Their God of Good was revealed in the New Testament and was concerned with brotherly love, charity and the spirit. They denied the virgin birth, crucifixion, and the resurrection on the ground that Christ was purely a spirit. They believed in the transmigration of souls and that all would eventually attain salvation either after this life or after reincarnation.

Christianity teaches:

1. That all men are born sinners.

2. That man can be saved from his sinful nature and inherit eternal life by accepting Jesus Christ as his own personal Saviour.

3. That God is the creator, sustainer, and preserver of the universe.

4. That the Bible is inspired of God and is the sole rule of faith and practice.

5. That every believer is his own priest.

6. That there are three persons in the Godhead – the Father, the Son, and the Holy Spirit, called the Trinity.

7. That the local church was established to be a witness of the saving power of Christ and to train and instruct the believers.

8. That there are two ordinances in the local church – baptism and the Lord's Supper. Baptism is a symbol of the death, burial and resurrection of Christ. The Lord's Supper is a symbol of the death of Christ.

9. That the Holy Spirit indwells every believer from the moment of his conversion.

10. That Christ was born of a virgin, lived a sinless life, was tried, crucified, buried and rose again; ascended to His Father where He is now seated on His right hand to be the intercessor of the believer; is coming again to judge the world.

ROMAN CATHOLICISM

CHAPTER 10

ROMAN CATHOLICISM

Roman Catholicism grew out of Christianity. The Catholic dogma that the Roman Catholic Church is the true church of Jesus Christ is without any foundation in fact.

The first two centuries of the Christian era was a period in which the churches remained true to the teaching of Christ and the apostles. Then there was a decline in Christianity when pagans were invited and accepted into the Christian Church, opening the way for the development of Roman Catholicism as we know it today.

Catholicism attempts to trace its system of popes back to Peter whom it claims as the chief apostle and the first pope. There is no supremacy given to Peter in Scripture. He is on an equality with all the other apostles. In fact, it was the Apostle Paul, not Peter, whom God used to spread the teachings of Christ throughout the world. It was Paul who established the early Christian churches and who instructed the early converts of Christianity.

During 314-335 A.D. when Silvester I was Bishop of Rome, Christianity was virtually made the state religion of the Roman Empire. The church then assumed an important place in politics. Constantine set himself up as the head of the church.

The Roman Empire was divided into two separate empires in 395. This made it difficult for one bishop to rule both empires.

Leo I (440-61) saw his opportunity to use the controversies between the East and West to seek to unify the empire under one head. He persuaded Atilla, the Hun, to spare the city of Rome and then induced Genseric, the Vandal, to have mercy on the city. This enhanced his reputation. Leo claimed that he was by divine right Primate of all bishops and proclaimed himself Lord of the whole church.

The Western Empire fell in 476, which left the pope free from civil authority. The pope was becoming the most commanding figure in the West.

Gregory I (590-604) was actually the first pope of Catholicism.

He came into power during a time of political anarchy and great public distress throughout Europe. He established complete control over the churches of Italy, Spain, Gaul and England. He labored unceasingly to purify the church. He opposed the practice of simony (sale of offices) and disposed of unworthy bishops. In his personal life, he was one of the best and purest popes.

Zacharias (741-52) made Pepin, the father of Charlemagne, King of the Franks. Stephen II (752-7) sent him with an army into Italy and conquered the Lombards and gave their land to the pope. This was the beginning of the Papal States.

Leo III (795-816) conferred on Charlemagne the title of Roman Emperor and Charlemagne gave him temporal power over the papal state. Charlemagne was one of the greatest influences in bringing the papacy to a postion of world power. In his 46-year reign, he waged many wars and conquests of Germany, France, Switzerland, Austria, Hungary, Belgium and parts of Spain and Italy.

Nicolas I (858-67) was the first pope to wear a crown. He used a false book which was circulated in 857 called the *Pseudo-Isidorian Decretals*. This was supposed to contain documents and letters of the bishops and councils of the second and third centuries which tended to exalt the power of the popes.

The darkest period in the history of the church was 870-1050 when bribery, corruption, immorality and bloodshed brought shame on the papacy.

The period of the harlots came into the papacy in 904-963. Sergius III (904-11) had a mistress, Marozia, who with her mother, Theodora, filled the papal chair with their illegitimate sons. John X (914-28) was brought from Ravenna to Rome and made pope by Theodora. He was smothered to death by Marozia. John XII (955-63), a grandson of Marozia, was guilty of almost every crime – violating virgins and widows, living with his father's mistress. He made the papal chair a brothel. While in the act of adultery, he was killed by the woman's enraged husband.

Boniface VII (984-5) murdered Pope John XIV. Benedict VIII (1012-24) bought the office of pope with open bribery. John XIX (1024-33) was a layman who passed through all the degrees of the clergy in one day and bought the papal chair. Benedict IX (1033-45) became pope when he was 12 years old, through a money bargain with the powerful families of Rome. He was a criminal engaged in robbery and finally the people of Rome drove him out of town.

Gregory VII (1073-85) sought to reform the papacy. He insisted on the celibacy of the clergy to cure their immorality and resisted the right of the emperors to appoint church offices to cure the practice of simony.

Anti-popes arose who were appointed by various emperors. Sometimes there were three or four popes who each claimed the right to the papal chair. Wars and much bloodshed went on among the claimants to the papacy. The crusades were conducted when the church was forced to fight the Mohammedans who were set on conquering the world.

Innocent III (1198-1260) was the most powerful pope of all time. He claimed to be the "Vicar of Christ" and claimed the right to depose kings and princes. He brought the church into supreme control of the state. He decreed transubstantiation, auricular confession, papal infallibility, forbade the reading of the Bible in the vernacular, ordered the extermination of heretics (non-catholics), instituted the inquisition, and ordered the massacres of the Albigenses (the true Christians of this period).

Boniface VIII (1294-1303) declared that all must belong to the Catholic Church in order to be saved.

The seat of the papacy was moved from Rome to Avignon, France, during the reign of Benedict XI (1303-4). In Avignon for 70 years, burdensome taxes were imposed, church offices were sold and many new offices were created to be sold. To protect their own families, the men of the community insisted on the priests keeping concubines.

There were two popes (1377-1417); one in Rome and one in Avignon. Each claimed to be the "Vicar of Christ."

John XXIII (1410-15) was the most depraved criminal to occupy the papal chair. The Catholics attempted to disown him until the recent pope took the same name and number in order to omit him from the list of popes. But he still held the papal chair.

Nicolas V (1447-55) authorized the King of Portugal to wage war on the African nations, take their property, and enslave their people.

Pius II (1458-64) had many illegitimate children and taught young boys his methods of seduction.

Sixtus IV (1471-84) decreed that money would gain the release of souls from purgatory.

Innocent VIII (1484-92) had sixteen children by various married women. He ordered the extermination of the Waldenses (the Bible believers of his day).

The Protestant Reformation was conducted when Leo X (1513-

21) was pope. He was made an archbishop at eight, a cardinal at thirteen. He issued indulgences for fees and declared the burning of heretics a divine appointment.

Paul III (1534-49) was a determined enemy of Protestants and offered Charles V an army to exterminate them.

Gregory XIII (1572-85) celebrated in a solemn mass with thanksgiving and joy the news of St. Bartholomew's massacre.

Leo XII (1821-29) condemned all religious freedom, tolerance, Bible societies and Bible translations. He declared that everyone separated from the Catholic Church will have no part in eternal life.

Pius IX (1846-78) decreed papal infallibility; proclaimed the right to suppress heretics (non-catholics) by force; condemned the separation of church and state; commanded all true Catholics to obey the head of the church rather than the civil rulers; decreed the immaculate conception and deified Mary; encouraged the superstitious regard for relics and declared that Protestantism is in no form a part of the Christian religion.

Leo XIII (1878-1903) claimed that he was appointed to be head of all rulers and that he held upon the earth the place of Almighty God. He pronounced Protestants as the enemies of the Christian name. He denounced "Americanism." He decreed that the only method of cooperation is complete submission to the Roman Pontiff.

The Catholic Church has retained some of the doctrines of Christianity such as the creation, the virgin birth of Christ, the crucifixion, ascension and resurrection of Christ, the sinfulness of man, the Trinity and the existence of heaven and hell. They have added dogmas which must be believed by all Catholics. These have no basis in Christianity and include such dogmas as papal infallibility, immaculate conception of Mary, the eternal virginity of Mary, Mary as the Mother of God, bodily ascension of Mary, transubstantiation, use of relics and images, baptism for the remission of sins, the priesthood, purgatory and extreme unction. Many of these dogmas have been incorporated from the other religions which we have studied.

The papacy is an Italian institution as it was built on the ruins of the Roman Empire. There were three methods which were used to bring the papacy to power: (1) political alliances, (2) deception as the Forged Decretals, and (3) armed force. The papal state has amassed large revenues by selling church offices and has been able to maintain the most luxurious court in Europe.

Some of the popes have been good men, some of them have been evil, but nearly all of them have been concerned with obtaining secular power. Most of the saints within the Catholic Church have been outside of the Vatican.

The chief cornerstone of Roman Catholicism is its teaching that it is the only true church as founded by Jesus Christ. History as well as Scripture repudiates this claim.

The Catholics have elevated Mary, the mother of Jesus, to a higher place than her son, who was sent as the Redeemer of the world. Mary has in practice assumed a place of deity which is unknown in Scripture.

The Catholics have built a system which has held its followers from birth (baptism) to death (extreme unction) in subjection to its teachings.

Confession is made before the priests rather than before God who alone has the power of forgiveness. "If we confess our sins, he [Jesus] is faithful and just to forgive us our sins and to cleanse us from all unrighteousness" (I John 1:9).

Roman Catholicism is a system based upon works rather than upon faith as taught in God's Word.

The Catholics had many sacraments which they claimed gave inward grace to the recipient. Gradually over the years the number has been reduced to seven which are practical in the Roman Church today.

1. Baptism of the new born child which Catholics claim takes away original sin and gives the child a modicum of free will or ability to do good.

2. Confirmation, or laying on of hands, at adolescence, to claim the individual for God. This is similar to the Sacred Thread ritual of Hinduism.

3. The Eucharist or sacrament of the Lord's Supper. Catholics claim that Christ is actually present in the wafer and the wine and call this transubstantiation.

4. Confession followed by penance. At first this was voluntary, but after 1215 it was required at least once a year.

5. Extreme Unction is the anointing with oil of the sense organs, loins and feet. This is supposed to remove any sin which has been committed. Still the recipient goes to purgatory to be cleansed of his sin, which Extreme Unction is supposed to forgive.

6. Holy Orders are performed for each priest by the bishop.

7. Marriage, which makes the union of man and woman and childbearing legitimate for the laity.

When the Roman Empire began to break up, the church at first separated itself from secular control and then seized temporal as well as spiritual authority. It claimed the right to govern all true Christians. It taught that the church was supreme rather than subject to king and emperor. The pope declared that he was the supreme judge, administrator and lawgiver; the final interpreter of the Scriptures and possessor of the keys of heaven itself. The church levied taxes and administered justice, using excommunication as its most potent penalty for violations. A whole new code of "canon law" was developed. Canon law was applied to all trials of the clergy and to all offenses against the church, such as heresy, atheism, adultery and sacrilege. The church became the center of social life. The church directed all education, dispensed all charity, controlled all the universities and book publishers, and conducted all hospitals. The church had charge of all the family records — marriages, divorces, births, deaths, wills, etc. The clergy considered themselves as agents of God to guide man's thought and actions. The church maintained that it controlled the entrance to heaven.

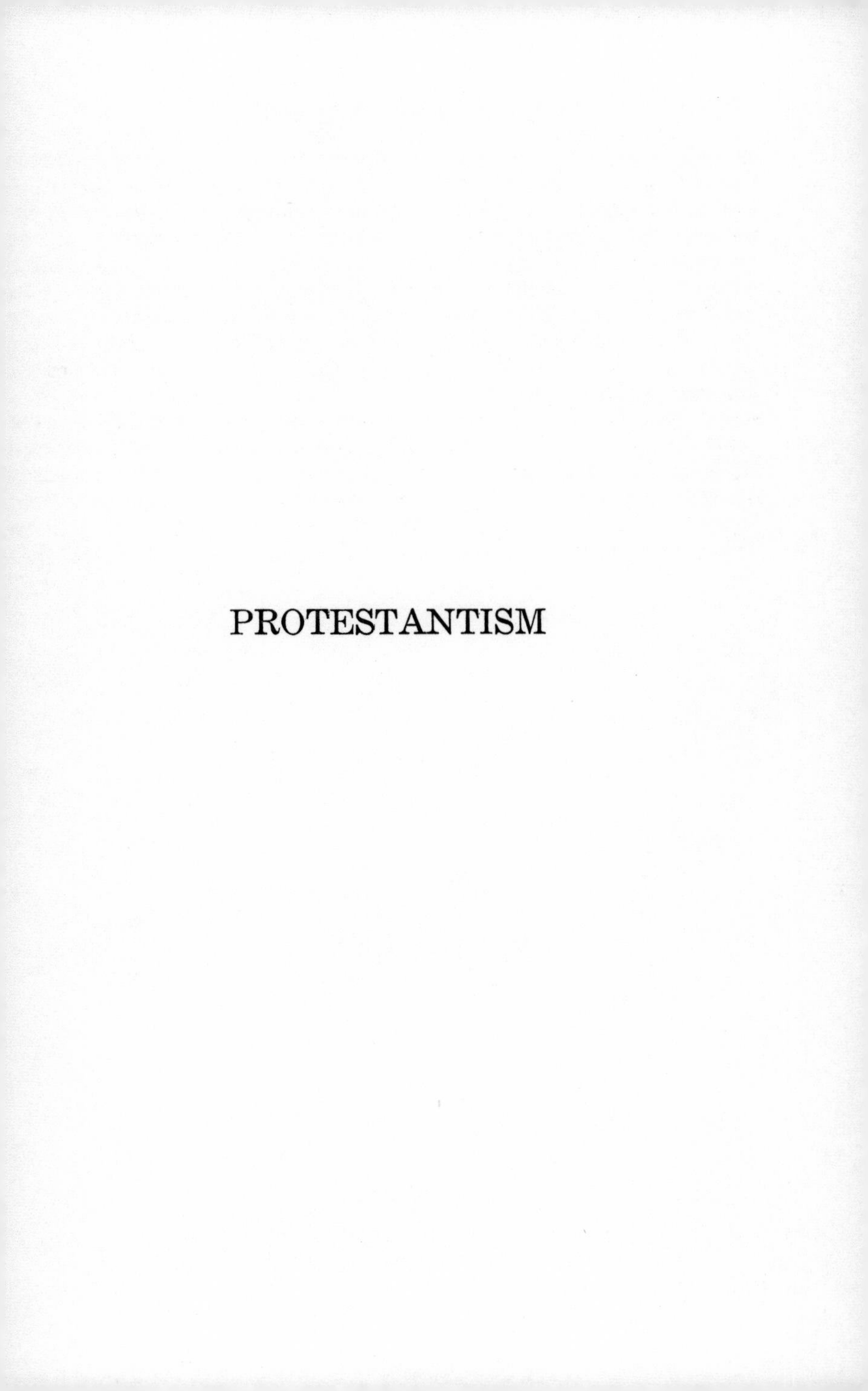

PROTESTANTISM

CHAPTER 11

PROTESTANTISM

At the time when the Roman Catholic Church held almost absolute sway over the peoples of Europe, Protestantism was a movement to return to the teachings of Christianity. Protestantism dates from the sixteenth century when Martin Luther, an Augustinian monk, broke from the Catholic Church in an effort to reform some of the abuses within his church.

The Protestant Reformation has been called a revolt by the Catholics, although the name Protestant was given to the reformers because they were "protesting" the dogmas and practices of the Catholic Church.

There were many attempts at reforming the Catholic Church before the time of Luther.

Martin Luther was the son of poor peasant Germans, but he received a good education. Although he attended law school, he quit the study of law and entered a monastery to become a monk.

He was appointed Professor of Philosophy at the University of Wittenberg when he was twenty-five. While teaching in the university he preached in the university church and studied the organization of the Christian Church.

Luther was a devout Roman Catholic, but he saw many things about the behavior of the pope and clergy with which he did not approve. He particularly objected to the selling of indulgences as being un-Christian and evil.

Luther made a trip to Rome and learned that Rome was not the holy city which he expected. He saw the people of Rome living shameful lives, while the pope was living in a castle surrounded by wealth, served as a king. Luther saw the people coming to the pope, kissing his feet, and begging favors of him. This was not the teaching of the humble Christ.

Luther returned to Wittenberg, an unhappy man. His experience in Rome had convinced him that the entire government of the Catholic Church was wrong.

Pope Leo X succeeded Julius II. Leo wished to outdo all the previous popes and he decided to build a church, the like of which had never been built before. He sent agents throughout the world to sell indulgences to raise the money to build the church.

Leo hired professional tradesmen to help the clergy in selling indulgences at a commission of 33⅓ per cent.

Luther wrote a number of letters to priests in Germany, asking them to protest against the selling of indulgences. The priests were afraid to interfere with the program of the pope. They knew the power and cruelty of the Inquisition.

Johan Tetzel was the pope's agent in Germany selling indulgences.

Luther appeared before the castle church at Wittenberg on October 31, 1517, and nailed his 95 theses protesting the practices of the Catholic Church. He invited public debate on his theses.

Luther's protests had an immediate effect on the sale of indulgences, which fell off drastically. This angered the pope and he issued a papal bull to throw Luther out of the clergy and to prohibit anyone from reading his writings. A copy of the bull was sent to Luther. This he burned in public and caused the final break between himself and the Church of Rome.

Luther had many admirers and followers who encouraged him to continue with his protests. He lectured and wrote more than 400 books and pamphlets. He translated the Bible into German, preached and organized the churches that broke away from the Church of Rome. His teachings spread beyond Germany into Norway, Sweden and Denmark.

He wrote, "The Church of Rome, formerly the most holy of all churches, has become the most lawless den of thieves, the very kingdom of sin, death and hell."

There were other men who were determined to reform the Catholic Church, but Luther was the most successful in focusing the attention of the world upon the abuses of the church.

Near the end of the twelfth century, Peter Waldo, a religious wealthy merchant, translated the Bible into French. He became convinced from the Scriptures that the pope and his followers were not living according to the teaching of Jesus. Also convinced that his own life as a wealthy merchant was not in accordance with the teaching of the Gospel, he gave his wealth to the poor and began to preach the Gospel of Christ from the New Testament. His sermons attracted a number of followers who called themselves Waldenses. After Waldo's death, his followers carried on his work. The pope prohibited them from preaching and ordered the Waldenses persecuted and killed wherever found.

John Wycliffe was a professor at Oxford in the fourteenth century. He arose as an opponent to the pope's power over England. He denied the absolute infallibility of the pope and criticized many of his practices. Objecting to the sermons and services of the church in Latin, he organized a number of priests who agreed with him and sent them to preach throughout England. He translated the Bible into English so that all the people could read and understand it. His work was suppressed in England but his influence reached into Germany and Bohemia and influenced the thinking of many of the young reformers.

Ulrich Zwingli, son of Swiss farmers, was given a good education and became a chaplain in the army. He settled in Zurich where he assumed a pastoral position. Switzerland was more advanced in democratic ideas than most of Europe, and Zwingli was permitted to introduce changes into his church which would not have been tolerated elsewhere. Married at the age of 40, Zwingli made his first break with the Catholic Church when he opposed the celibacy of the priests. He attacked the worship of idols and led in the removal of all pictures, crucifixes and images from the churches of Zurich.

John Calvin was born in 1509 in Noyon, seventy miles from Paris. He entered the University of Paris at 14 after he had exhausted all the learning in Noyon. He spent four years in the university where he distinguished himself for his scholarship. He studied religion, law, Hebrew, Greek and the Classics. He studied for five years after leaving the university, still uncertain as to what career to follow. Three years later he wrote *The Institutes of the Christian Religion* which established him as one of the most important religious writers on Christianity. Protestants were being burned at the stake, so Calvin fled from France to Switzerland for refuge. He lived nearly all his life in Geneva where he devoted himself to the writing of Protestant works and the organization of Protestant churches. His teachings were known as Calvinism and spread over Europe, taking root throughout the world.

John Knox preached Protestantism in Scotland. He had to flee Scotland for his safety and went to Geneva where he became acquainted with Calvin and his teachings. He returned to Scotland and established the church on a Calvinistic basis except for some minor differences. His church was called Presbyterian and became one of the larger denominations.

The pope of Rome had sent Augustine to England in 597 A.D. to convert the Saxons to Catholicism. Several hundred years later, this church wanted to break its ties with Rome. It did not object to the religion of the pope but to his political power. In 1534 the head of the Church of England resolved that the pope of Rome had no greater authority in England than any other foreign bishop. The Church of England broke away from Rome, but its beliefs, ritual and ministry remained almost the same as Roman Catholicism. It is known in America as the Protestant Episcopal Church.

The Anabaptists appeared soon after the spread of the teachings of Peter Waldo. They were already many in number when Luther and Zwingli separated from Roman Catholicism. They differed from Luther and Zwingli because they did not believe in infant baptism. Over two thousand Anabaptists were executed from 1517-1530. The Anabaptists were the forerunners of the Baptists and Congregationalists and were opposed by both the Protestants and Catholics.

Protestant denominations began to multiply steadily, each one differing from the other in some of their beliefs and practices. There is, however, a unity of belief in many of the cardinal doctrines of Christianity through the many denominations.

There are so many denominations in America now bidding for the attention of the people that the question, "What church should I join?" arises. It must be remembered, however, that church membership is not essential to salvation, but each believer should be a member of a local church where his testimony will be united with other Christians for the spread of the Gospel. Christians need the fellowship of others of like mind and a home base from which to work.

Dr. R. A. Torrey, a noted Bible teacher, gave some suggestions to guide the believers in choosing the right church. He wrote, "Unite with a church where they believe in the Bible and where they preach the Bible. Avoid the churches where words are spoken, open or veiled, that have a tendency to undermine your faith in the Bible as a reliable revelation from God Himself, the all-sufficient rule of faith and practice. Unite with a church where there is a spirit of prayer, where the prayer meetings are well kept up. Unite with a church that has a real, active interest in the salvation of the lost, where young Christians are looked after and helped, where minister and people have a love for the poor and outcast, a church that regards its mission in this world to be the same as the mission of Christ, to seek and to save the lost.

"As to denominational differences, other things being equal, unite with that denomination whose idea of doctrines and government and of the ordinances are most clearly akin to your own. But it is better to unite with a live church of some other denomination than to unite with a dead church of your own. . . . Denominational differences are becoming ever less and less, and oftentimes they are of no practical consequence whatsoever; and one will often feel more at home in a church of some other denomination than in any accessible church of his own denomination. The things that divide the denominations are insignificant compared to the great fundamental truths and purposes and faith that unite them.

"If you cannot find a church that agrees with the patterns set forth above, find the church that comes nearest to it. Go into that church and by prayer and by work try to make it as nearly as you can like the pattern for the church of Christ. But do not waste your strength in criticism against either church or minister. Seek that which is good in the church and in the minister and do your best to strengthen it. Hold aloof, firmly but unobtrusively, from what is wrong, and seek to correct it. Do not be discouraged if you cannot correct it in a day or a week or a month or a year. Patient love and prayer and effort will tell in time. Drawing off by yourself and snarling and grumbling will do no good. That will simply make you and the truths for which you stand repulsive."

During the last one hundred and fifty years, a number of sects or cults have developed in America which are classified as Protestant but are in no way connected with the Reformation. They are non-Christian groups and must be classified as neither Protestant nor Catholics. Many of these groups are spreading from America to the other countries of the world.

The Church of Jesus Christ of Latter-day Saints, commonly called the Mormons, was founded by Joseph Smith in 1830.

Mary Baker Eddy established the Christian Science Church in 1879.

Jehovah's Witnesses was founded by Charles Taze Russell in 1879.

Theosophy was founded by Madame Blavatsky in 1875.

Unity was founded by Myrtle and Charles Fillmore in 1889.

Many other cults are being developed which attract large followings and spread their teachings.

Many of the Protestant denominations have been divided into countless groups differing in some minor doctrine or practice so that today we find many different Baptist, Methodist, etc., groups.

Protestantism has placed the emphasis upon several doctrines which can be traced through all the various Christian denominations.

The Supreme Authority of the Bible. The Bible as the infallible Word of God is the infallible guide for faith and practice of the Protestant. This is in opposition to the supreme authority of the pope in Catholicism. The Bible was translated into the languages of the people of the world so that they could read and understand it for themselves. This promoted literacy as the people were taught to read and write that they might be able to read the Scriptures. The Bible is often the first book to be translated into another language.

The unmediated Lordship of Jesus Christ. Salvation is obtained through faith in Jesus Christ. One of the formal principles of Protestantism is justification by faith as opposed to the doctrine of works. Nearly all the religions of the world, including Catholicism, have devised a scheme of salvation by works. Complete redemption is the work of God through Christ who was sent as the Sinbearer of the sinner. He is the Substitute for the sins of the world. The sinner works after his salvation, but he cannot work to obtain his salvation. This is the free gift of God.

Jesus Christ is the sovereign Lord of the Church and of the world. Christ founded the Church.

Forgiveness may only be obtained through faith in Christ. The sinner must be united to Christ through the "new birth" experience of conversion, as Paul was an example in Acts 9 and as Jesus explained to Nicodemus in John 3.

The risen Christ is the perennial source of strength for the believer. The source of strength for the early apostles was the fact that Christ arose from the grave and is now seated on the right hand of God. The same source of strength is available now to the believer. The believer worships a living Saviour to whom he can go at all times for forgiveness and cleansing, for sympathy and for strength.

The Witnessing Responsibility of the Church. The supreme function of the Christian Church is to bear witness to God. The Church exists to witness the good news of human salvation in and through Jesus Christ. Witness must be borne to the Gospel by word and by life. The centrality of preaching, of proclaiming the Gospel by word, is one of the chief characteristics of Protestantism. The Gospel must be proclaimed with passionate conviction because it is true and because it is important and obedience to it is urgent.

The church is to bear witness by the pious lives of its members dedicated to Christ as personal Saviour.

There is a school of thought which has arisen within the rank of Protestantism which seeks to undermine the historic doctrines of Christianity. Although it is certainly not new, it is commonly called Modernism or Liberalism. There have always arisen groups who have sought to deny the teachings of Christianity.

Modernism must be judged on the basis of individuals who are teaching the modernist views within the Protestant churches. The Modernist preacher or teacher has found it to his advantage to work from within. Many modernist preachers have been ordained and remain in good standing in denominations which as a whole do not share their views. The early universities of our nation were founded by men and groups which adhered to the historic Christian doctrines, but a small group often led by one modernist teacher has succeeded in leading these schools from the path of truth into the denial of the faith. Many churches have been led from the truth of the New Testament into the errors of Modernism and have lost their power for good to God or their community.

Modernism has invaded all the Protestant denominations, although it has been kept in check more in some denominations than it has in others. Thus this work of destruction is more noticeable in some denominations than in others.

The modernist preachers and teachers follow a carefully prepared plan of destruction. First, they train their attack on the Bible. They deny that the Bible is the infallibly inspired Word of God and picture it as a great historical, literary work of man. Then they turn their attack to Jesus. They deny the literal interpretation of the chief events in the life of Christ as His virgin birth, His vicarious atonement, His resurrection. They portray Him as a great religious teacher in the same category as Buddha, Confucius, Lao-tze, and Mohammed, instead of as the Son of God as the Bible teaches. They seek to humanize Christ while they glorify man.

All modernist teachers and preachers do not agree on all points, but there are several points with which they are in agreement:

1. The divineness of all life.
2. The oneness of man with the eternal.
3. The essential goodness of human nature.
4. The rise of man through a process of evolution.
5. The reign of natural law.
6. Heaven and hell not as places but as conditions of the soul.
7. Character as the aim of religion.

Modernism stresses the social aspect of Christianity more than the spiritual. It has become popular because it lifts the ego of the average person, telling him what he wants to hear — how good he is — and not what he needs to know — that he is a sinner who needs to be saved through the vicarious atonement of Jesus Christ.

The Modernists have no organization such as a denomination, but they are interested in bringing all the Protestant denominations into their sphere of thinking. The Federal Council of Churches has been organized for this purpose. This organization boasts that it is the spokesman for American Protestantism. The leaders who have gained control of this group are Modernistic in theology. Denominational leaders who have led their denominations into this group are Modernists. It must be remembered, however, that not every church which belongs to a denomination which is a member of the Federal Council is modernistic, although a church which is in a denomination affiliated with the Federal Council should withdraw from the denomination to retain its Christian character and purpose.

Modernism is a dread disease within the Protestant Church which can only be corrected by the members of the church. Ministers must be carefully chosen on the basis of their convictions and adherence to the truth of the Word of God.

The chief emphasis of Protestantism is the personal acceptance of the gift of grace by the individual. Every believer who accepts Christ as his own personal Saviour is his own priest.

The Protestant congregation is regarded as a group of personally converted people which assembles together to witness to the saving power of Christ. Personal holiness is demanded of the Christian with a personal devotion to Christ.

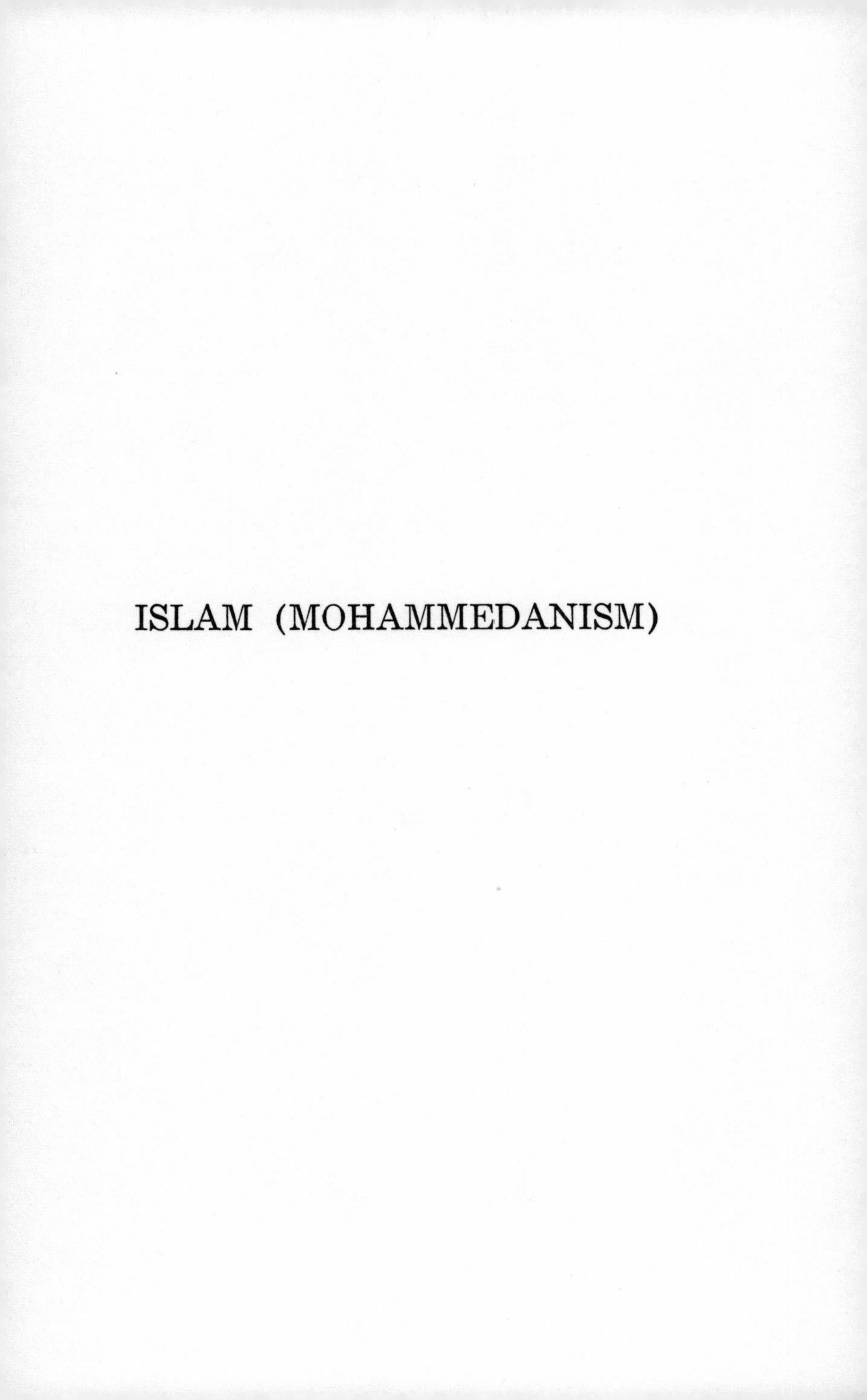

ISLAM (MOHAMMEDANISM)

CHAPTER 12

ISLAM (MOHAMMEDANISM)

Mohammedanism was founded by Mohammed ibn Abdullah who lived in the period of 570-632 A.D. Arabia was the birthplace of Mohammedanism.

The sacred book of Mohammedanism is the Koran which contains 114 chapters of Mohammed's revelations. These are not arranged topically nor in the order in which Mohammed received the revelations but are arranged according to length – the shortest first, the longest last.

Mohammedanism is also known as Islam, which means submission, and its followers are called Moslems, which means those who submit to its teachings.

Before the time of Mohammed, the Arabs were nature worshipers. They worshiped the sun and the stars which were divided into 360 idols – one for each day of the year as the Arab year has only 360 days. The main idol was Habel which was made in the form of a man chiseled out of red agate with one hand made of gold.

Arabia was divided into many clans and tribes and each tribe had idols and beliefs of its own.

Because of its geographical position, Arabia was never oppressed by the great power of the East and West. It teemed with beliefs in sacred stones, sacred palms, and sacred hills. It was known as "The Land of Incense." The people combined religion with business in the selling of incense, spices and perfumes in the market place of Mecca, when the people came to the temple to worship.

The merchants of Mecca claimed the Well of Ishmael as their private property and began to sell its water to the worshipers. Even in their ignorance the Arabians began to wonder if there was any holiness in its water sold as merchandise. They began to doubt the holiness of Zemzem, the holiness of Kaabs, and the divinity of their idols. They turned to gambling, drinking and fortune telling.

Mohammed was born of an aristocratic family in Mecca in 570 A.D. at the height of the gambling and drinking of the Arabs.

Both of Mohammed's parents died when he was six years old and he was taken into the home of an uncle, Abu Talit. His orphaned state gave Mohammed a certain objectivity and detachment of judgment. He looked on many of the beliefs and customs of his community with a critical appraisal which was born of questioning and distaste. He was disturbed by the incessant quarreling over religious matters among the Qurayph chiefs.

Mohammed was hired as a shepherd helper as soon as he was old enough. He spent his childhood on the edge of the desert. The desert was his school; the sun by day and the stars by night were his teachers.

Mohammed left sheep herding and became a camel driver. He led caravans laden with Arabian products that were to be sold in the markets of Egypt in the West, Persia in the East, and Syria in the North.

His reputation as a caravan leader gained Mohammed favor among the merchants of Mecca. The wealthy widow, Kadijah, employed him. He was sent with a caravan laden with spices and perfumes to Syria and was entrusted with the sale of merchandise and the purchases of silk and linen in exchange.

Mohammed married Kadijah, who was fifteen years his senior. They lived happily for fifteen years as their business prospered and their wealth increased.

The mixed idolatry of the people, great drunkenness, and the gambling depressed Mohammed. He often wondered what could be done to improve the conditions of his countrymen.

Mohammed had met many Jews and Christians on his caravan routes. He talked with many of them in the various marketplaces which he visited.

Mohammed could not read or write and Waraka, his wife's cousin, read the Bible to him. The New Testament story of Jesus convinced him that Arabia needed an inspired prophet and leader who could rescue the Arabs to faith in one God and lead them from their evil practices to the ways of a good life.

The Bible inspired Mohammed and he left the city and spent many hours brooding over conditions in his country and how they might be changed for the better. One day as Mohammed sat meditating, the angel Gabriel was supposed to have appeared to him with a golden tablet in his hands. Mohammed hurried home to tell his wife of his vision. Kadijah believed that Mohammed had actually talked with an angel and encouraged him to go out into the hills again and await new revelations from heaven. Gabriel was reported to have appeared again and again with new revelations.

Slowly the idea possessed Mohammed that he was a prophet chosen by God and he began to preach to his family and relatives. He gained several followers among his immediate family. He went to the sacred temple and preached to the people who had gathered there to worship their idols.

Mohammed was sensitive to ridicule. He preached again and again whenever he could find an audience. The belief in one God grew in his mind. The people ridiculed his teaching; he ignored them and went on with his preaching. He urged the people to turn from their idol worship to belief in one God, Allah. His admonitions about the people's gambling, drinking and fortune-telling only amused them.

He did not stop his attacks on the idolatry, drunkenness and gambling, but he began to preach against the rich merchants and the leaders of Mecca who used the Well of Ishmael and the Temple of the Kaabs as sources of profit. The merchants were incensed at his attacks and sent messages to Mohammed's family warning them to stop him from preaching against the corruption of the rich.

The messages of Mohammed were really messages of the beliefs of Judaism, Christianity and his own ideas of reform combined. His small group of followers called their religion Islam, which means submission to the commands of Allah. Mohammed's followers were called Moslems or True Believers.

The sermons and speeches of Mohammed were written down by one of his followers, Abu Bekr. The legislature passed an edict that any Arab who accepted Islam would be driven out of Mecca. The people were afraid to accept Islam.

Kadijah died and Mohammed was grief-stricken. He went to Talif, seventy miles from Mecca, to spread his teachings. Talif was the center of the grape growers and wine merchants who hated Mohammed. The people attacked him and drove him out of the city.

He returned to Mecca. Twelve pilgrims came from Yathrib, 270 miles from Mecca, and asked Mohammed to come to explain his teachings. There were many Jews in Yathrib who had heard of Mohammed's belief in one God and his hatred for idols, and they could understand his teachings for they had a common ground in their own beliefs.

In the next year, Mohammed gained seventy-five converts in Yathrib, from whom he chose twelve men whom he appointed apostles to spread the teachings of Islam.

The people of Mecca plotted against Mohammed. He fled from Mecca to Yathrib on his favorite camel, Al Kaswa. The night of his flight is the most important date in Islam's history. It is known as the Hegira – the night of the flight. They count the time on their calendars from A.H. (Anno Hegira, the year of the flight). Before the flight, Mohammed was the prophet of a new religion, but now he was the founder of its church.

He was received with open arms in Yathrib and proclaimed ruler of the city. The name of Yathrib was changed to Medina (city of the prophet).

Mohammed began to organize his religion, as he was not content just to reform the people of Mecca. He had the ambition and vision of reforming the people of the whole world.

Medina was a walled city surrounded by date orchards, and Mohammed and his followers could fortify themselves against hunger and their enemies.

He organized an army but he had the problem of feeding it. So he went into the desert and claimed that Gabriel instructed him to waylay and rob the caravans coming from Mecca and foreign lands. He was acquainted with the caravan routes because of his past experience as a caravan leader. The success of his plunder of the caravans convinced Mohammed that this was a sign that Allah was with him and his followers. Mohammed also wanted these attacks on the caravans to bring the merchants of Mecca out into the open.

The merchants came out into the open and hired soldiers to attack Mohammed. War was declared between Mecca and Medina.

Mohammed organized his forces to meet the attack. He gathered an army of 10,000 armed followers and marched to Mecca.

He stopped before each idol and said, "Truth is come and falsehood is fled away," as his followers smashed each idol. They did not plunder nor destroy anything in Mecca, except the idols. The Meccans came back from the hills where they had taken refuge during the attack. They accepted Islam when they saw that their homes and marketplaces had not been plundered.

Mohammed organized his forces to spread his teachings throughout the world. In three years he had conquered all of Arabia and many neighboring countries. His armies swept through Asia, Africa and much of Europe.

Mohammed delivered his last sermon to his followers when he was sixty-three years old. He told them:

"Keep the faith as is the will of Allah,

"Be kind to the poor,

"Give the laborer his wage before his perspiration is dry,
"Do not worship idols."

The teachings of Mohammed became the creed of Islam with few alterations or additions. The fundamentals of his faith are set forth in the Koran. It is easily understood by the masses.

The first part of the Moslem creedal formula reads, "[There is] no god but Allah." This is the most important article in Moslem theology. God is one and undivided. The most heinous sin to the Moslem is to associate any other being with God on terms of equality. God existed before any other being or thing. He is self-subsistent, omniscient, omnipotent, the creator and the sole arbiter who will save the believer out of dissolution of the world and place him in Paradise.

The Koran is not consistent in its portrayal of the character of Allah. If the Koran was arranged in chronological order, the different conception would be seen. Allah would become less Jewish and more Arabian. He would govern men less loosely and guide them more rigorously. There is an underlying conception of God's purpose to bring the world to judgment. The willful wickedness of man is in rebellion against the will of God. The God of mercy and love must in justice hold man responsible for acts which he has freely committed in contravention of God's holy will.

The second half of the Moslem creed reads: "Mohammed is the messenger (or prophet) of Allah." It is self-evident to the Moslem that God must reveal Himself through prophets – or else man could not know Him. God must not leave Himself without witnesses. There is a long line of prophets, including Abraham, Moses and Jesus, but Mohammed is the last and greatest of them all, the "seal" of those who appeared before him. None is his equal either in knowledge or in authority; none has received or handed down so perfect a revelation. His authority is supreme. He was not a divine being appearing in the flesh. He was human and he did not pretend to supernatural powers; he performed no miracles; he instituted no mystical sacraments; he ordained no holy priesthood. Modern theology has refused to deify Mohammed.

The five pillars of the religious duty of Mohammedanism are:

1. Recitation of the creed: There is no god but Allah and Mohammed is the prophet of Allah. This is the first step in becoming a Moslem and is heard everywhere in the Moslem world.

2. Prayer: Prayer is offered five times a day: at dawn, at midday, at mid-afternoon, at sunset, and at the fall of darkness. The worshiper goes through the ritual of ablution, rolls out his

prayer rug and bows down facing Mecca. Friday is the special day of public prayer for all adult males. The faithful assemble at the mosque under the leadership of the Imam at noon or sunset. The service at the Mosque is held in the paved courtyard. The pray-ers leave their shoes at the entrance and perform their ablutions of hands, mouth, nostrils, face, fore-arms, neck and feet at the pool or fountain. They hear the reader recite from the Koran. The Imam appears and the faithful take their places in long rows facing Mecca; they are spaced so as to allow their throwing themselves forward in prostration on their prayer mats. After the prayer, the Imam preaches a sermon having for its purpose the exposition of Moslem doctrine.

3. Almsgiving: Almsgiving is called Zakat and in the early days of Moslem history was a yearly tax similar to our income tax. It was paid in kind or money on every Moslem's property and income. It was gathered by the officials into a common treasury and was distributed in part as charity to the poor and used in part for the repair and administrative expenses of the Mosques. This fund was separate from the tribute exacted of non-Moslems for political and military expenses. Zakat was once universally obligatory but now in some regions is voluntary. No one is expected to neglect it on pain of exciting contempt.

4. Fast: During the sacred month of Ramadan, fast obligations are compulsory on all Moslems except the sick and ailing. The fast starts as soon as it is possible to distinguish between a white and black thread at dawn and ends when the threads are no longer distinguishable at dusk. No food or drink is to be taken during the fast.

5. Pilgrimage: Once in a lifetime of every Moslem – men and women – a pilgrimage is to be made to Mecca if at all possible. Moslems are expected to be in Mecca during the sacred month of Dhu'l-Hijja.

Mohammed unified the Bedouins for the first time in their history into a powerful military group. They were yoked together by their economic need and their religious faith.

FOR FURTHER STUDY

FOR FURTHER STUDY

Most of the books listed here may be borrowed from the public libraries of your community to enable you to further your study of the Religions of the World.

General

(containing articles on the various Religions of the World)

Archer, John Clark, *Faiths Men Live By* (T. Nelson and Sons, New York, 1934).
Ashby, Philip H., *The Conflict of Religions* (Scribner's Sons, New York, 1955).
Berry, Gerald L., *Religions of the World* (Barnes and Noble, Inc., New York, 1947).
Bouquet, Alan Coates, *The Christian Faith and Non-Christian Religions* (Harper, New York, 1958).
Braden, Charles Samuel, *The World's Religions* (Cokesbury Press, Nashville, 1939).
Browne, Lewis, *This Believing World* (Macmillan Co., New York, 1930).
Burtt, Edwin Arthur, *Man Seeks the Divine* (Harper, New York, 1957).
Clarke, James Freeman, *Ten Great Religions* (Houghton-Mifflin and Co., Boston, 1899).
Das, Bhagavan, *The Essential Unity of All Religions* (Indian Book Shop, Benares, India, 1947).
Fairchild, Johnson E., *Basic Beliefs* (Sheridan House, New York, 1959).
Ferm, Vergilius, *Ancient Religions* (Philosophical Library, New York, 1950).
———, *Living Schools of Religion* (Littlefield College, Ames, Iowa, 1958).
———, *Religion in the Twentieth Century* (Philosophical Library, New York, 1948).
Fitch, Florence, *Their Search for God* (Lothrop, Lee and Shepard, New York, 1947).
Gaer, Joseph, *How the Great Religions Began* (New Amercian Library of World Literature, New York, 1956).
Hopkins, Edward Washburn, *The History of Religion* (The Macmillan Co., New York, 1918).
Hume, Robert Ernest, *The World's Living Religions* (C. Scribner's Sons, New York, 1952).
Jurji, Edward J., *The Great Religions of the Modern World* (Princeton University Press, Princeton, N.J., 1946).
Kitagawa, Joseph Mitsuo, *Religions of the East* (Westminster Press, Philadelphia, 1960).
Landis, Benson Young, *World Religions* (Dutton, New York, 1957).
Life, "The World's Great Religions" (Time, Inc., New York, 1957).
Lyon, Quinter Marcellus, *The Great Religions* (Odyssey Press, New York, 1957).

Menzies, Allan, *History of Religion* (C. Scribner's Sons, New York, 1903).
Moore, George Foot, *The Birth and Growth of Religion* (C. Scribner's Sons, New York, 1913).
Noss, John Boyer, *Man's Religions* (Macmillan Co., New York, 1956).
Parkes, James William, *Common Sense About Religion* (Macmillan Co., New York, 1961).
Potter, Charles Francis, *The Faith Men Live By* (Prentice-Hall, New York, 1954).
Ring, George Cyril, *Religions of the Far East* (Bruce, Milwaukee, 1950).
Smith, Huston, *The Religions of Man* (Harper, New York, 1958).
Soper, Edmund Davison, *The Religions of Mankind* (Abingdon-Cokesbury Press, New York, 1951).
Spiegelberg, Frederic, *Living Religions of the World* (Prentice-Hall, Englewood, Cliffs, N.J., 1956.
Toynbee, Arnold Joseph, *Christianity Among the Religions of the World* (Scribner's Sons, New York, 1957).
Van Buskirk, William Riley, *The Saviors of Mankind* (The Macmillan Co., New York, 1929).

HINDUISM

Ananda, Acharya, *Brahmadarsanam; or Intuition of the Absolute* (The Macmillan Co., New York, 1917).
Barnett, Lionel David, *Hindu Gods and Heroes* (J. Murray, London, 1922).
Bernard, Theos, *Hindu Philosophy* (Philosophical Library, New York, 1947).
Borequet, Allan C., *Hinduism* (Longmans, Green and Co., New York, 1950).
Farquha, J. N., *An Outline of the Religious Literature of India* (Oxford University Press, New York, 1920).
Griswold, H. D., *Insights Into Modern Hinduism* (Henry Holt and Co., New York, 1934).
Garbe, Richard, *India and Christendom* (Open Court Publishing Co., La Salle, Illinois, 1959).
Griffith, R. T. H., *The Hymns of the Rig Veda* (E. J. Lazarus and Co., Benares, India, 1895).
Griswold, H. D., *The Religion of the Rig Veda* (Oxford University Press, New York, 1923).
Guenon, Rene, *Introduction to the Study of the Hindu Doctrines* (Luzac and Co., London, 1945).
Keith, A. B., *The Religion and Philosophy of the Vesta and the Upanishads* (Harvard University Press, Cambridge, Mass., 1920).
Macnical, N., *Hindu Scriptures* (Everyman's Library, J. M. Dent and Sons, n.d.).
McKenzie, John, *Hindu Ethics* (Oxford University Press, New York, 1922).
Monier-Williams, M., *Brahmanism and Hinduism* (Macmillan and Co., New York, 1891).
Morgan, Kenneth William, *The Religion of the Hindus* (Ronald Press Co., New York, 1953).
Nikhilananada, *Hinduism* (Harper, New York, 1958).
O'Malley, L. S. S., *Popular Hinduism, the Religion of the Masses* (Macmillan and Co., New York, 1935).
Pratt, J. B., *India and Its Faiths* (Houghton-Mifflin and Co., Boston, 1915).
Radhakrishnan, S., *The Philosophy of the Upanishads* (Allen and Unwin, London, 1924).

Sarma, D. S., *Hindu Renaissance* (Benares Hindu University, Benares, India, 1944).
Schweitzer, Albert, *Indian Thought and Its Development* (Henry Holt and Co., New York, 1936).
Shil-ponde, *Hindu Astrology* (Willey Book Company, New York, 1944).
Soper, Edmund Davison, *The Inevitable Choice: Vendanta Philosophy or Christian Gospel* (Abingdon Press, New York, 1957).
Spalding, Baird, *Life and Teaching of the Masters of the Far East* (California Press, San Francisco, 1924).
Valniki, *The Adventures of Rama* (Little, Brown & Co., Boston, 1954).
Renon, Louis, *Hinduism* (G. Braziller, New York, 1961).

BUDDHISM

Anesaki, Masaharu, *The History of Japanese Religion* (Kegan, Paul, Trench, Trueboner Co., London, 1931).
Beck, Mrs. L., *The Splendour of Asia: the Story and Teaching of the Buddha* (Dodd Mead and Co., New York, 1926).
Blofeld, John, *The Jewel in the Lotus: an Outline of Present-Day Buddhism in China* (Buddhist Society, London, 1948).
Brown, Brian, *The Story of Buddha* (David McKay Co., Philadelphia, 1927).
Carus, Paul, *The Gospel of Buddha* (Open Court Publishing Co., Chicago, 1917).
Coomaraswamy, Ananda, *Hinduism and Buddhism* (Philosophical Library, New York, 1943).
———, *Buddha and the Gospel of Buddhism* (G. P. Putnam's Sons, New York, 1916).
Davids, T. W. Rhys, *Buddhist India* (G. P. Putnam's Sons, New York, 1903).
Davids, T. W. Rhys and Caroline A., *Sacred Books of the Buddhist* (Macmillan and Co., New York, n.d.).
Davids, Mrs. T. W. Rhys, *A Manual of Buddhism* (Macmillan and Co., New York, 1932).
Eliot, Sir Charles, *Japanese Buddhism* (Edward Arnold, London, 1935).
———, *Hinduism and Buddhism*, 3 vols. (Edward Arnold, London, 1921).
Evans, Wentz, *Tibetan Yoga and Secret Doctrines* (Oxford University Press, New York, 1935).
Gard, Richard Abbott, *Buddhism* (G. Braziller, New York, 1961).
Goddard, Dwight, ed., *A Buddhist Bible* (Dwight Goddard Estate, Thetford, Vermont, 1938).
Grant, Frances Ruth, *Oriental Philosophy* (Dial Press, New York, 1936).
Herold, A. F., *The Life of Buddha* (Boni and Liveright, New York, 1927).
Humphreys, Christmas, *The Wisdom of Buddhism* (Random House, New York, 1960).
Johnson, R. F., *Buddhist China* (E. P. Dutton, New York, 1913).
Keith, A. B., *Buddhist Philosophy in India and Ceylon* (Clarendon Press, Oxford, 1923).
Moore, Charles A., ed., *Philosophy–East and West* (Princeton University Press, Princeton, N.J., 1944).
Noble, Margaret, *Myths of the Hindus and Buddhists* (Henry Holt and Co., New York, 1914).
Otto, Rudolph, *Mysticism – East and West* (Macmillan and Co., New York, 1932).

Pratt, J. B., *The Pilgrimage of Buddhism* (Macmillan and Co., New York, 1928).
Reichelt, K., *Truth and Tradition in Chinese Buddhism* (Commercial Press, Shanghai, 1934).
Reischauer, A. K., *Studies in Japanese Buddhism* (Macmillan and Co., New York, 1917).
Saunders, Kenneth J., *Gutama Buddha* (Association Press, New York, 1920).
Shinran, *Buddhist Psalms* (J. Murray, London, 1921).
Simpson, William, *The Buddhist Praying Wheel* (Macmillan Co., New York, 1896).
Smith, Vincent A., *Asoka — the Buddhist Emperor of India* (Oxford University Press, New York, 1920).
Suttapitaka, *Sayings of Buddha* (Columbia University Press, New York, 1908).
Suzuki, D. T., *Outlines of Mahayana Buddhism* (Luzac, London, 1907).
———, *Essays in Zen Buddhism* (Luzac, London, 1928).
Thomas, Edward J., *The History of Buddhist Thought* (Alfred A. Knopf, New York, 1934).
———, *The Life of Buddha* (Alfred A. Knopf, New York, 1927).
Warren, Henry Clarke, *Buddhism in Translation* (Harvard University Press, Cambridge, Mass., 1922).
Wright, Arthur F., *Buddhism in Chinese History* (Stanford University Press, Stanford, Calif., 1959).
Zachibana, S., *The Ethics of Buddhism* (Oxford University Press, New York, 1926).

JAINISM

Jaini, J., *Outlines of Jainism* (Cambridge University Press, Cambridge, Mass., 1916).
Stevenson, Mrs. Sinclair, *The Heart of Jainism* (Oxford University Press, New York, 1915).

CONFUCIANISM

Brown, Brian, *The Story of Confucius* (David McKay Co., Philadelphia, 1927).
Creel, Herrlee Glessner, *Confucius, the Man and the Myth* (J. Day Co., New York, 1949).
Crow, Carl, *Master Kung* (Harper and Brothers, New York, 1938).
Giles, Lionel, *The Sayings of Confucius* (Wisdom of the East Series, John Murray, 1917).
Hughes, E. R., *Chinese Philosophy in Classical Times* (Everyman's Library, J. M. Dent, 1941).
Johnson, R. F., *Confucianism and Modern China* (Appleton-Century Crofts, New York, 1935).
Kaijuka, Shigeki, *Confucius* (Macmillan Co., New York, 1956).
Legge, James, *The Works of Mencius* (Clarendon Press, Oxford, 1895).
Lin Yutang, *The Wisdom of Confucius* (The Modern Library, Random House, New York, 1938).
Lin, Wu-chi, *Confucius, His Life and Time* (Philosophical Library, New York, 1955).
Lyall, Leonard A., *The Sayings of Confucius* (Longmans, Green, New York, 1925).
———, *Mencius* (Longmans, Green, New York, 1932).

Moore, Charles A., *Philosophy – East and West* (Princeton University Press, Princeton, N.J., 1944).
Waley, Arthur, *The Analects of Confucius* (Allen and Unwin, London, 1938).
Wilhelm, Richard, *Confucius and Confucianism* (Harcourt, Brace, New York, 1931).
Wang, Kung-hsing, *The Chinese Mind* (John Day Co., New York, 1946).

SHINTOISM

Anesaki, M., *The Religious Life of the Japanese People* (Tokyo, 1938).
———, *History of Japanese Religion* (London, 1930).
Aston, W. G., *Shinto: the Way of the Gods* (Longmans, Green and Co., New York, 1905).
Ballou, R. O., *Shinto: the Unconquered Enemy* (Viking Press, New York, 1945).
Holtom, D. C., *Modern Japan and Shinto Naturalism* (University of Chicago Press, Chicago, 1943).
———, *The National Faith of Japan* (E. P. Dutton and Co., New York, 1938).
Kato, Genchi, *A Study of Shinto: the Religion of the Japanese Nation* (Tokyo, 1926).
Ono, Montonori, *Shinto, the Kami Way* (Bridgeway Press, Rutland, Vt., 1961).
Wheeler, Post, *The Sacred Scriptures of the Japanese* (H. Schuman, New York, 1952).

TAOISM

Dubs, H. H., *China* (University of Chicago Press, Chicago, 1946).
Giles, H. A., *Chuang Tzu – Mystic, Moralist and Social Reformer* (Kelly and Walsh, Shanghai, 1926).
Giles, Lionel, *The Sayings of Lao Tzu* (John Murray, New York, 1905).
———, *Taoist Teachings of the Book of Leih Tzu* (Wisdom of the East Series, London, 1925).
———, *Musings of a Chinese Mystic* (Wisdom of the East Series, London, 1925).
Goodrich, L. C., *A Short History of the Chinese People* (Harper and Co., New York, 1943).
Hughes, E. R., *Chinese Philosophy in Classical Times* (Everyman's Library, New York, 1950).
Latourette, K. S., *The Chinese, Their History and Culture* (Macmillan and Co., New York, 1934).
Legge, James (translator), *The Texts of Taoism* (Sacred Books of the East Series, Clarendon Press, Oxford, 1891).
Tsui Chi, *A Short History of Chinese Civilization* (G. P. Putnam's Sons, New York, 1943).
Tzu, Lao, *That Way of Life* (The New American Library, New York, 1955).
Waley, Arthur, *The Way and Its Power, a Study of the Tao Te Ching* (Allen and Unwin, London, 1934).
———, *Three Ways of Thought in Ancient China* (Allen and Unwin, London, 1931).
———, *The Way and Its Power* (Houghton-Mifflin, Boston, 1935).
Wei, Francis C. M., *The Spirit of Chinese Culture* (Charles Scribner's Sons, New York, 1947).
Yang, Y. C., *China's Religious Heritage* (New York and Nashville, 1943).

Yutang, Lin, *The Wisdom of China and India* (Random House, New York, 1942).
Welch, Holmes, *The Parting of the Way* (Beacon Press, Boston, 1957).

ZOROASTRIANISM

Dhalla, M. N., *History of Zoroastrianism* (Oxford University Press, New York, 1938).
———, *Zoroastrian Civilization* (Oxford University Press, New York, 1922).
Jackson, A. V. W., *Zoroaster, the Prophet of Ancient Iran* (Columbia University Press, New York, 1898).
———, *Zoroastrian Studies* (Columbia University Press, New York, 1928).
Masani, Rustom Petonji, *The Religion of the Good Life* (G. Allen and Unwin, London, 1938).
Pavry, Jal Dastur Cursetji, *The Zoroastrian Doctrine of the Future Life* (Columbia University Press, New York, 1926).
Zaehner, Robert Charles, *The Dawn and Twilight of Zoroastrianism* (Putnam, New York, 1961).

JUDAISM

Asch, Sholem, *What I Believe* (G. P. Putnam's Sons, New York, 1941).
Baeck, Leo, *Essence of Judaism* (New York, 1936).
Bamberger, Bernard Jacob, *The Story of Judaism* (Union of American Hebrew Congregations, New York, 1957.
Barack, Nathan A., *Faith for Fallibles* (Bloch Publishing Co., New York, 1952).
Baron, Salo Wittmayer, *A Social and Religious History of the Jews* (Columbia University Press, New York, 1952).
Bentwich, Norman De Mattos, *Israel* (McGraw-Hill Book Co., New York, 1952).
Berger, Elmer, *A Partisan History of Judaism* (Devin-Adair Co., New York, 1951).
Bernstein, Philip Sidney, *What the Jews Believe* (Farrar, Straus and Young, New York, 1951).
Bevan and Singer, editors, *The Legacy of Israel* (Clarendon Press, Oxford, 1927).
Browne, Lewis, ed., *The Wisdom of Israel* (Random House, New York, 1945).
Cohen, Abraham, *Everyman's Talmud* (J. M. Dent and Sons, London, 1932).
Cohen, Samuel S., *What We Jews Believe* (Union of American Hebrew Congregations, Cincinnati, Ohio, 1931).
Finegan, Jack, *Light From the Ancient Past* (Princeton University Press, Princeton, N.J., 1946).
Eisentein, Ira, *Creative Judaism* (Behrman House, New York, 1941).
———, *Judaism* (London, 1939).
Finkelstein, Louis, *The Jews: Their History, Culture, and Religion* (Harpers, New York, 1949).
———, *Judaism – the Religion of Democracy* (Devin-Adair Co., New York, 1941).
Fitch, Florence Mary, *One God, the Ways We Worship Him* (Lothrop, Lee and Shepard Co., 1944).
Frank, Waldo, *The Jew in Our Day* (Duell, Sloan and Pearce, New York, 1944).
Friedlander, Michael, *The Jewish Religion* (New York, 1935).
Gaer, Joseph, *Our Jewish Heritage* (Henry Holt, New York, 1957).

Goldberg, Israel, *Fulfillment: the Epic Story of Zionism* (World Publishing Co., New York, 1951).
Goldin, Judah, *The Living Talmud— the Wisdom of the Fathers* (New American Library, New York, 1957).
Goodman, Paul, *A Histroy of the Jews* (E. P. Dutton Co., New York, 1919).
Gordis, Robert, *Judaism for the Modern Age* (Farrar, Straus and Cudahy, New York, 1955).
Herberg, Will, *Judaism and Modern Man* (Farrar, Straus and Young, New York, 1951).
Heschel, Abraham Joshua, *Between God and Man* (Harper, New York, 1959).
———, *God in Search of Man* (Farrar, Straus and Cudahy, New York, 1955).
———, *Man Is Not Alone* (Farrar, Straus and Young, New York, 1951).
Isserman, F. M., *This Is Judaism* (Willett, Clark and Co., Chicago, 1944).
Kac, Arthur W., *The Rebirth of the State of Israel* (Moody Press, Chicago, 1958).
Kaplan, Mordecai M., *The Meaning of God in Modern Jewish Religion* (Behrman's Jewish Book House, New York, 1937).
———, *Judaism As a Civilization* (Behrman's Jewish Book House, New York, 1934).
Kertzer, Morris Norman, *What Is a Jew?* (World Publishing Co., Cleveland, 1953).
Kittel, Rudolph, *The Religion of the People of Israel* (Macmillan and Co., New York, 1925).
Kligerman, Aaron J., *Messianic Prophecy in the Old Testament* (Zondervan Publishing House, Grand Rapids, 1957).
Kohler, Kaufmann, *Jewish Theology Systematically and Historically Considered* (Macmillan and Co., New York, 1918).
Lindberg, Milton B., *Witnessing to Jews* (American Messianic Fellowship, Chicago, 1948).
———, *The State of Israel and the Jews Today in the Light of Prophecy* (American Messianic Fellowship, Chicago, 1930).
———, *The Jews and Armageddon* (American Messianic Fellowship, Chicago, 1940).
Meek, T. J., *Hebrew Origins* (Harper and Co., New York, 1936).
Morgenstern, Julian, *A Jewish Interpretation of the Book of Genesis* (Cincinnati, 1919).
Morris, Joseph, *Judaism as Creed and Life* (London, 1903).
Noyes, Carleton Eldredge, *The Genius of Israel* (Houghton-Mifflin Co., Boston, 1924).
Oesterley, W. O. E. and Robinson, T. H., *The Hebrew Religion: Its Origin and Development* (Macmillan Co., 1937).
Peters, John P., *The Religion of the Hebrews* (Ginn and Co., Boston, 1914).
Philipson, David, *The Reform Movement in Judaism* (The Macmillan Co., New York, 1931).
Pool, David de Sola, *Why I Am a Jew* (T. Nelson, New York, 1957).
Roth, Leon, *Judaism: a Portrait* (Viking Press, New York, 1961).
Sachar, H. L., *A History of the Jews* (Alfred A. Knopf, Inc., New York, 1930).
Schechter, Solomon, *Some Aspects of Rabbinic Theology* (New York, 1909).
Silver, Abba Hillel, *Where Judaism Differed: an Inquiry Into the Distinctiveness of Judaism* (Macmillan, New York, 1956).
Simonhoff, Harry, *Under Strange Skies* (Philosophical Library, New York, 1953).

Singer, Isidore, *A Religion of Truth, Justice and Peace* (The Amos Society, New York, 1924).
Steinberg, Milton, *Basic Judaism* (Harcourt, Brace, New York, 1947).
Wouk, Herman, *This Is My God* (Doubleday, Garden City, N.Y., 1959).

CHRISTIANITY

Berkhof, L., *Systematic Theology* (Wm. B. Eerdmans Publishing Co., Grand Rapids, 1959).
Baillie, John, *What Is Christian Civilization?* (Charles Scribner's Sons, New York, 1948).
Buswell, J. O., *Systematic Theology* (Zondervan Publishing House, Grand Rapids, 1962).
Butterfield, Herbert, *Christianity and History* (George Bell and Sons, Ltd., London, 1949).
Calvin, John, edited by David Otis Fuller, *Instruction in Christianity* (Wm. B. Eerdmans Publishing Co., Grand Rapids, 1947).
Carnell, Edward John, *A Philosophy of the Christian Religion* (Wm. B. Eerdmans Publishing Co., Grand Rapids, 1952).
Evans, William, *The Great Doctrines of the Bible* (Moody Press, Chicago, 1912. Revised 1949).
Keyser, Leander S., *A Philosophy of Christianity* (The Luthern Literary Board, Burlington, Ia., 1948).
Mullins, E. Y., *Christianity at the Crossroads* (George H. Doran Co., New York, 1924).
Smith, Wilbur M., *Therefore Stand* (W. A. Wilde Co., Boston, 1945).
Turner, J. Clyde, *These Things We Believe* (Convention Press, Nashville, 1956).
Wallace, Ronald S., *Calvin's Doctrine of the Word and Sacrament* (Wm. B. Eerdmans Publishing Co., Grand Rapids, 1957).

ROMAN CATHOLOCISM

Aldama, Manuel Garrido, *From Roman Priest to Radio Evangelist* (Zondervan Publishing House, Grand Rapids, 1946).
Anderson, S. E., *Is Rome the True Church?* (Zondervan Publishing House, Grand Rapids, 1958).
Berkouwer, G. C., *Recent Developments in Roman Catholic Thought* (Wm. B. Eerdmans Publishing Co., Grand Rapids, 1958).
Blanshard, Paul, *American Freedom and Catholic Power* (Beacon Press, Boston, 1949).
———, *The Irish and Catholic Power* (Beacon Press, Boston, 1953).
Carder, James L., *Methods of Witnessing to Romans Catholics* (The Fundamental Press, Chicago, 1944).
Carrara, John, *Why a Preacher and Not a Priest?* (Zondervan Publishing House, Grand Rapids, 1937).
———, *Catholicism Under the Searchlight of the Scriptures* (Zondervan Publishing House, Grand Rapids, 1943).
———, *Should Protestants and Roman Catholics Intermarry?* (Zondervan Publishing House, Grand Rapids, 1953).
Chiniquy, Charles, *Fifty Years in the Church of Rome* (Baker Book House, Grand Rapids, 1958).
Crowley, Jeremiah J., *Romanism – a Menace to the Nation* (The Menace Publishing Co., Aurora, Missouri, 1912).

Deane, L. Earl, *Catholicism Judged by the Bible* (Zondervan Publishing House, Grand Rapids, 1959).
Fradryssa, G. V., *Roman Catholicism Capitulating Before Protestantism* (Southern Publishing Co., Mobile, Alabama, 1908).
Fulton, Justin, *Why Priests Should Wed* (Protestant Book House, Toledo, Ohio, 1927).
Hampel, Harry, *My Deliverance From the Heresies of Rome* (Harry Hampel, Dallas, Texas).
———, *How to Win Catholics to Christ* (Harry Hampel, Dallas, Texas).
———, *Salvation Through the Catholic Bible* (Harry Hampel, Dallas, Texas).
King, L. J., *House of Death and Gate of Hell* (Protestant Book House, Toledo, Ohio, 1932).
Macaulay, J. C., *The Bible and the Roman Church* (Moody Press, Chicago, 1946).
McLaughlin, Emmett, *People's Padre* (Beacon Press, Boston).
———, *American Culture and Catholic Schools* (Lyle Stuart, New York, 1961).
———, *Crime and Immorality in the Catholic Church* (Lyle Stuart, New York, 1962).
O'Gorman, Edith, *Convent Life Unveiled* (Scottish Protestant League, Glasgow).
Peterson, F. Paul, *The Rise and Fall of the Roman Catholic Church* (The Convert, Clairton, Pa., 1960).
Pike, James, *A Roman Catholic in the White House* (Doubleday and Company, Garden City, New York, 1960).
Price, Oliver W., *The Bible and the Church – Which Came First?* (Dunham Publishing Co., Findlay, Ohio, 1958).
Vila, Manuel Perez, *I Found the Ancient Way* (Moody Press, Chicago, 1958).
Woods, Henry M., *Our Priceless Heritage* (Evangelical Press, Harrisburg, Pa., 1941).
Zacchello, Joseph, *Ins and Outs of Romanism* (Christian Literature Depot, Winnipeg, Man., 1950).

PROTESTANTISM

Bach, Marcus, *Report to Protestants* (Bobbs-Merrill Co., Indianapolis, 1948).
Berkhof, Louis, *Recent Trends in Theology* (Wm. B. Eerdmans Publishing Co., Grand Rapids, 1944).
Boyer, Merle William, *Luther in Protestantism Today* (Association Press, New York, 1958).
Brown, William Adams, *The Church, Catholic and Protestant* (C. Scribner's Sons, New York, 1935).
Cobb, John B., *Varieties in Protestantism* (Westminster Press, Philadelphia, 1960).
Dillenberger, John, *Protestant Christianity Interpreted Through Its Development* (Scribner's Sons, New York, 1954).
Garrison, Winfred Ernest, *A Protestant Manifesto* (Abingdon-Cokesbury Press, New York, 1952).
Herberg, Will, *Protestant, Catholic, Jew* (Doubleday, Garden City, New York, 1955).
Kerr, Hugh Thomson, *Positive Protestantism* (Westminster Press, Philadelphia, 1950).
Lawton, J. S., *Conflict in Christology* (Society for the Propagation of Christian Knowledge, London, 1947).

Henry, Carl F. H., ed., *Contemporary Evangelical Thought* (Channel Press, Great Neck, New York, 1957).
———, *Fifty Years of Protestant Theology* (W. A. Wilde Co., Natick, Mass., 1950).
———, *The Protestant Dilemma* (Wm. B. Eerdmans Publishing Co., Grand Rapids, 1949).
Machen, J. Gresham, *Christianity and Liberalism* (Macmillan Co., New York, 1925).
Underwood, Kenneth Wilson, *Protestant and Catholic* (Beacon Press, Boston, 1957).
Van Til, Cornelius, *The New Modernism* (Presbyterian and Reformed Publishing Co., Philadelphia, 1947).

MOHAMMEDANISM

Ameer, Ali, *The Spirit of Islam* (MacClelland and Stewart, Toronto, 1935).
Ali, Mohammed, *The Religion of Islam* (Lahore, India, 1936).
Andrae, Tor, *Mohammed: the Man and His Faith* (Chas. Scribner's Sons, New York, 1936).
Arnold and Guillaume, *Legacy of Islam* (Clarendon Press, Oxford, 1931).
Arnold, T. W., *The Preaching of Islam* (Constable and Co., London, 1913).
Barton, James Levi, *The Christian Approach to Islam* (The Pilgrim Press, Boston, 1918).
Bengalee, M. R., *Life of Mohammed* (Moslem Sunrise Press, Chicago, 1941).
Bodley, Ronald V. C., *The Messenger: the Life of Mohammed* (Doubleday and Co., New York, 1946).
Cragg, Kenneth, *Sandals at the Mosque* (Oxford University Press, New York, 1959).
Fairs, Nabih Amin, ed., *Arab Heritage* (Princeton University Press, Princeton, N.J., 1944).
Fernan, Friedrich Welhelm, *Moslems on the March* (Knopf, New York, 1954).
Fitch, Florence Mary, *Allah, the God of Islam* (Lothrop, Lee and Shepard, New York, 1950).
Gibb, H. A. R., *Modern Trends in Islam* (University of Chicago Press, Chicago, 1947).
———, *Mohammedanism: a Historical Survey* (Oxford University Press, New York, 1949).
Goldzicher, I., *Mohammed and Islam* (Yale University Press, New Haven, Conn., 1917).
Hitti, P. K., *History of the Arabs* (Macmillan and Co., New York, 1937).
Houtsma, M., ed., *Encyclopedia of Islam* (London, 1913).
Hurgronje, Christiaan Snonck, *Mohammedanism* (G. P. Putnam's Sons, New York, 1916).
Irving, Washington, *Life of Mohomet* (Dutton, New York, 1911).
Levy, Ruben, *The Sociology of Islam*, 2 vols. (Williams and Norgate, London, 1930).
Lincoln, Charles Eric, *The Black Muslims in America* (Beacon Press, Boston, 1961).
Margoliouth, D. S., *Mohammed and the Rise of Islam* (G. P. Putnam's Sons, New York, 1905).

Mohammed, Iqbol, *The Reconstruction of Religious Thought in Islam* (Oxford University Press, New York, 1934).
Morgan, Kenneth William, *Islam: the Straight Path* (Ronald Press Co., New York, 1958).
Pool, John J., *Studies in Mohammedanism* (Archibald Constable, London, 1892).
Lammers, Henri, *Islam: Beliefs and Institutions* (London, 1929).
Schroeder, Eric, *Mohammad's People* (Bond Wheelwright Co., Portland, Me., 1955).
Smith, Wilfred Cantwell, *Islam in Modern History* (Princeton University Press, Princeton, N.J., 1957).
Stoddard, Theodore Lothrop, *The New World of Islam* (C. Scribner's Sons, New York, 1921).
Wensinck, A. J., *The Muslim Creed* (Cambridge, 1932).
Williams, John Alden, *Islam* (G. Braziller, New York, 1961).
Palmer, E. H., translator, *The Koran* (Oxford, 1928).
Zwemer, Samuel M., *Across the World of Islam* (Fleming H. Revell Co., New York, 1929).
———, *The Influence of Animism on Islam* (The Macmillan Co., New York, 1920).